MAKIN' YOUR OWN

Country Instruments

ANDY dePAULE

OLIVER PRESS
WILLITS, CALIFORNIA

Library of Congress Card Number 75-34754
ISBN 0-914400-23-1

Cover by Bruce McCloskey

First Printing July 1976

OLIVER PRESS
1400 Ryan Creek Road
Willits, California 95490

MAKIN' YOUR OWN

CONTENTS

FOREWORD

Many times people ask me how I learned to make instruments. They wonder, did I have a long apprenticeship? They have a hard time believing that I just picked it up.

ANYBODY CAN!!! It is not hard to make instruments. You don't have to sweep the master's floor for ten years while he drops you a "secret" here and there. It is all just common sense and practice. Stir in a little patience, add a few wood shavings, and you have a "guitar stew" or a "fiddle gumbo."

It won't cost you much to make an instrument. You should be able to make any instrument in this book for around $25. Some may cost $10 more, some less. If you take your time and do it right, you should wind up with a valuable instrument worth quite a bit of money.

For instance, you can make a guitar for about $30 that will be better sounding than a $500 factory-made guitar. It can be a lot fancier, too. It's all up to you.

"But I don't have many tools," you say. Hey, dig this . . . you can make the instruments in this book with a few common wood-working tools.

A few months ago, I was in a town down in Mexico where everybody makes guitars. You would be surprised to see how nice an instrument they make with a handful of tools and a small working space.

"But won't I need some special tools and jigs that will cost a lot of money?" you may ask. Yes, you will need a few tools that might be expensive if you bought them. But you can make these tools yourselves very cheaply, and I'm going to show you how.

"Doesn't it require expensive, exotic, imported wood to make instruments?"

Baloney! You can make fine instrments out of domestic lumber. Many Luthier companies sell economically priced instrument wood and supplies.

When I first started making guitars, I was afraid I would botch the whole thing, so naturally I didn't want to invest a lot of money. I understand how you feel. I felt the same way. However, if you follow the instructions in this book exactly, you will wind up with a fine instrument for next to nothing.

It sure feels good to play an instrument that you made for yourself, and hear someone ask, "Hey, that guitar sure sounds good. Is that a Martin?"

"Hell, no," you say. "This is a John Doe Special, extra deluxe custom-made, the only one in the world!"

WOOD AND HUMIDITY

Wood for the Face of the Instrument

The face is the single most important part of any string instrument. Traditionally, German spruce is the wood to use, but remember—traditions were made before the discovery of America. In this country many kinds of soft wood are available that are suitable for making fine instruments. Two of them are Western red cedar and Canadian yellow cedar. Both of these are very similar to German spruce in texture and tone value. Also, Sitka spruce (the best of which grows in Alaska) is a common wood found in instruments, and all of the major guitar companies use it exclusively.

WOOD FOR GUITAR

Now here is where a division occurs in this book. Do you have a band saw available to you or not? If not, you will have to send away for the wood for the face. There are many companies which sell supplies for instrument makers (some are listed in the back of this book). These companies have various grades of European and domestic spruce. The difference in the wood has (to them) more to do with looks than actual wood quality. For example, the cheap spruce will have "defects" such as wide or uneven grain, curly figures in the wood or small knots (which can be avoided), or dark annual lines. These woods can still be used to make fine instruments. If you have a band saw you can cut your own wood. What you will need for the face is straight grained, vertical spruce or cedar...the size will depend on the instrument you are building. Figure No. 1 shows the log and the section that is needed. First the log must be split (quartered) with a froe. Next you cut the quartered log on a band saw, making the following cuts. These cuts are approximately 1/4".

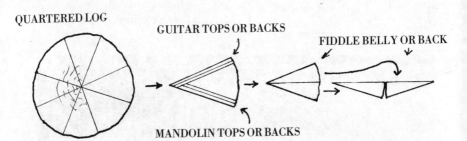

QUARTERED LOG

GUITAR TOPS OR BACKS

FIDDLE BELLY OR BACK

MANDOLIN TOPS OR BACKS

When you split the wood out of a log, the drawback is that even if the log is well aged, the thin face wood cut from it will need to be air dried for another year or so to make certain that it is really dry.

Cutting the Face from a Board

The best thing you can do is to get a board of the right width for the instrument being made and rip it on the band saw. When choosing wood, look for a vertical grain wood board. The board should look like this:

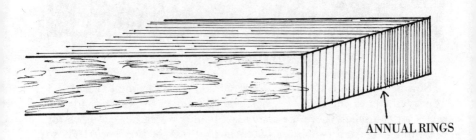

ANNUAL RINGS

A good way to check and double check the board after you have picked it out is to chip two corners and see how they break off. A clean split is no good, as it indicates slash grain. A rough break is good, as this would indicate a vertical grain with the fibers going straight through the board.

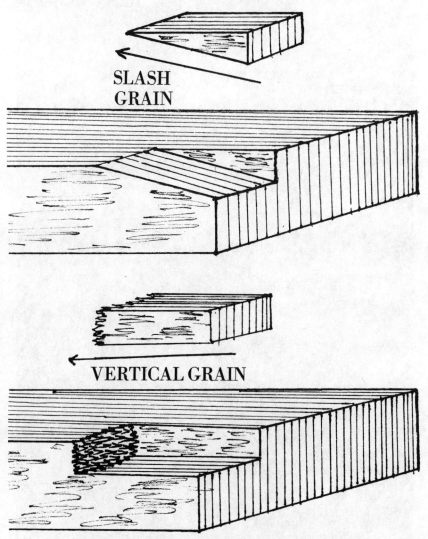

SLASH GRAIN

VERTICAL GRAIN

Always take a plane with you when you are shopping for wood....you have to see what you are buying. (If I get lost in a wood mill, you can find me by following the wood shavings!!!)

Cutting on the Band Saw

It will be necessary to set up a guide wall when cutting wood so thin (Figure No. 7). This guide can be made from old 2 by 8 board.

RIPPING WOOD WITH GUIDE WALL

5

You will make a cleaner cut with a wide new saw blade. I use a 1/2" skip tooth blade for ripping (four teeth per inch). It is also best to run the saw as slowly as possible.

When you start cutting the wood, test your guide set-up on a piece of scrap wood first, to see if it is cutting an even thickness across the full width of the board. Push the wood through the saw slowly to get a cleaner cut and also to keep the blade as sharp as possible for as long as you can. (Friction caused by pushing the wood too hard will cause the blade to lose its set and temper.) Also when you get near the end of the cut, you will need to push it the rest of the way with a stick. If you accidentally cut the end off of one of your fingers, it will be hard to play when you have finished your instrument. Clean the pitch off the blade after each cut with a rag soaked in kerosene.

Wood for Backs and Sides

WOOD FOR FIDDLE

WOOD FOR GUITAR BACK

The nicest wood for guitar backs and sides is Brazilian rosewood, and flamed maple is good for fiddles, but they are very expensive and hard to get. Another commonly used wood is bird's-eye, or even plain straight grain maple is nice. Another wood is black walnut, which sometimes has beautiful figures and which is my second choice after rosewood. The list of woods you could use is never ending......any well-cured wood will do.

If you choose to use a hard wood for the back and sides, you will either have to buy a set (back and sides) from a luthier supply house, or cut it on a band saw. If you cut it yourself, you can get boards cheaper than sets. The board you cut will have to be thick enough to get all the pieces you need. You must remember that you will lose about 1/16" with each cut. Japanese guitars use plywood backs and sides. So do some American guitars—even name brands. If you wish to save a good amount of money, you can do this by buying plywood door skins and using them. An instrument made with plywood backs and sides will not sound a good as one made with solid wood, but if you spend a lot of time on the face, and do a good job with that, you should still come up with a good sounding instrument. Fiddles have to be made from solid wood, as they are carved.

Wood for the Necks

Honduras mahogany is most often used for guitar necks, and maple for fiddles and mandolins; however, almost any good, well seasoned hard wood will do for any instrument. Walnut is a nice substitute, or you could use beech wood, birch or what have you. Necks can be carved from solid blocks or built up if the wood is not available in block form.

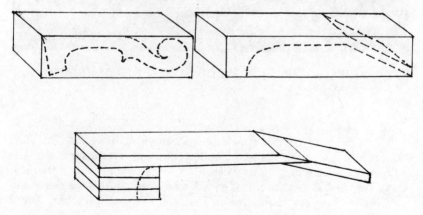

Wood for the Linings

Bass wood is very good for linings and is very easy to use, but many other woods can be used: i.e., mahogany, spruce, maple or willow. Linings are the strips of wood inside instruments which provide the gluing surface to hold the top and back to the sides.

"Bracings"—[Faces]

One of the most important parts of a string instrument is the bracing in the face of an instrument. Aside from giving the face the strength it needs to hold up for many years, it is also the factor that controls the tone of the instrument. The best woods for bracing faces are spruce or cedar. For bracing backs, use mahogany or maple.

RIPPING BRACING WOOD FOR VERTICAL GRAIN

Getting Your Wood From the Forest

If you plan to continue making instruments, it is wise to start collecting a good supply of wood, and cutting your own insures that you will have a good supply. You will need a large chain saw and wedges, and a froe and axe are useful. You will also need an Alaskan chain mill attachment for your chain saw so that you can make lumber. These

8

attachments are sold commercially for about $80.00 and up, but you can make the one in the following diagram for about $5.00 or less, and it works just as well. The materials that you will need are listed below:

One (1) 2'' x 6'' board, the same length as your saw blade
One (1) 1/2'' x 18'' all thread, cut in half
Eight (8) 1/2'' lock washers
Four (4) 1/2'' washers
Four (4) 1/2'' wing nuts
Four (4) 1/2'' nuts (hexagon)

As shown in the diagram, the wing nuts are used to set the depth of the cut. For the first cut, you will need to nail two 2 by 4 boards along the length of the log, one on each side. These guide the saw straight for the first cut.

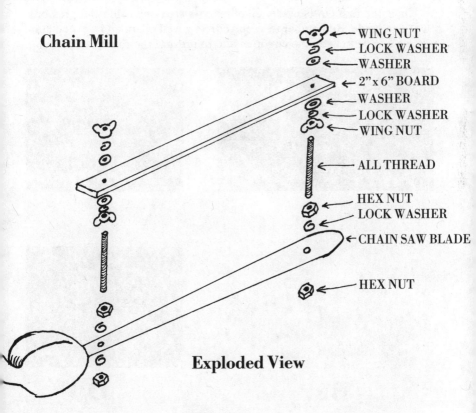

Chain Mill

← WING NUT
← LOCK WASHER
← WASHER
← 2" x 6" BOARD
← WASHER
← LOCK WASHER
← WING NUT

← ALL THREAD

← HEX NUT
← LOCK WASHER
← CHAIN SAW BLADE

← HEX NUT

Exploded View

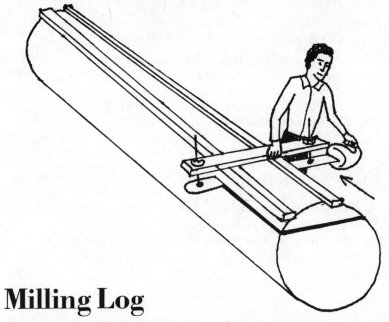

Milling Log

Once the first cut is made, all other cuts are done using the previous cut as a guide. Remember to keep your saw well oiled, and on long cuts use a wedge to keep the cut open and to prevent the saw from binding.

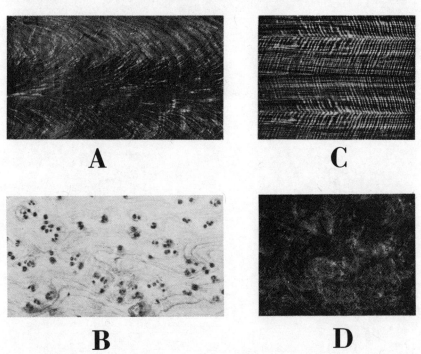

A

C

B

D

Choosing a Tree

In cutting cedar or spruce trees for face wood, look for a tall tree at least 30 inches in diameter. Avoid a tree with lots of branches or knots, as you want clear wood. When cutting hardwood for backs, sides and necks, look for the features that you want in the wood by studying the outside of the tree. Most wood is straight grained. But often you find a tree with figured wood, such as: A. crotch; B. bird's-eye; C. flamed (curley grain) of D. burl, as shown. The following drawings show how to judge a tree for figured grain. Once you have chosen the trees you want, you are ready to start.

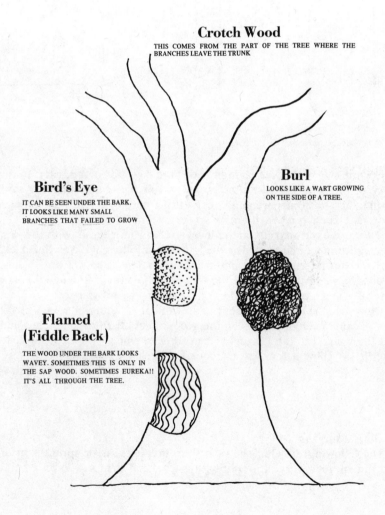

Crotch Wood

THIS COMES FROM THE PART OF THE TREE WHERE THE BRANCHES LEAVE THE TRUNK

Bird's Eye

IT CAN BE SEEN UNDER THE BARK. IT LOOKS LIKE MANY SMALL BRANCHES THAT FAILED TO GROW

Burl

LOOKS LIKE A WART GROWING ON THE SIDE OF A TREE.

Flamed (Fiddle Back)

THE WOOD UNDER THE BARK LOOKS WAVEY. SOMETIMES THIS IS ONLY IN THE SAP WOOD. SOMETIMES EUREKA!! IT'S ALL THROUGH THE TREE.

Falling a Tree

In falling, you must be thoughtful of where you want the tree to fall. Even though this is a simple operation, you must pay attention. If a tree is already leaning in one direction, then that is where you should fall it. If it is straight up and down, then fall it to a place where it will be easy to mill. Now follow the steps shown in the diagram.

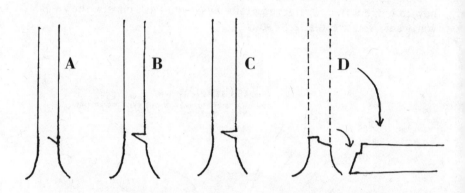

A. On the side of the tree facing the desired direction of fall, cut into the base of the trunk (as close to the ground as possible) with your saw; coming up at a 30 degree angle, cut a little more than half way through the tree. Then remove the saw.
B. Now make the next cut on the level so that you meet up with the first cut, and remove the saw. The wedge should fall right out with a kick.
C. Now cutting in from the other side of the tree about 2 or 3 inches above the wedge, cut in until the tree starts to creak. Remove the saw carefully and put it aside. Don't take your eye off the tree.
D. Now give the tree a good shove and while it is falling, get back as far as you can. When the tree is on the ground, cut off all the branches and cut the trunk into the lengths you need. Remember when cutting it to lengths to allow a few extra inches for checking.

Milling Your Log

The following drawing shows how to mill a cedar or spruce log for instrument tops. First it is split with a froe, and then sawed on a band saw.

12

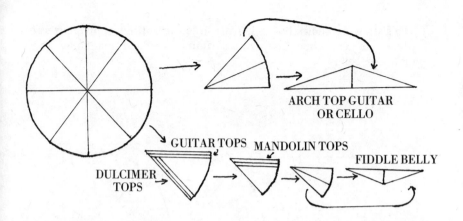

ARCH TOP GUITAR
OR CELLO

GUITAR TOPS   MANDOLIN TOPS

DULCIMER
TOPS

FIDDLE BELLY

This drawing shows how a hardwood log is first sawed into planks and then split (quartered) to produce a variety of wood for assorted instruments. The first few cuts are about 4 inches deep, and then as you near the center of the log, cuts are 2 inches. When the center is reached, the rest of the log is split (quartered).

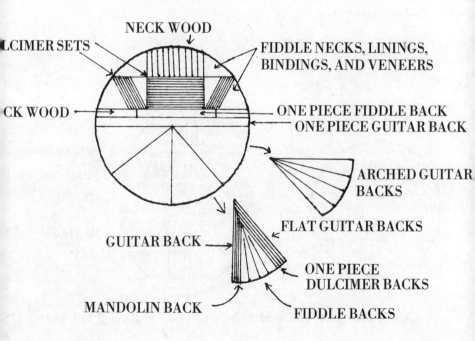

NECK WOOD

LCIMER SETS

FIDDLE NECKS, LININGS,
BINDINGS, AND VENEERS

CK WOOD

ONE PIECE FIDDLE BACK
ONE PIECE GUITAR BACK

ARCHED GUITAR
BACKS

FLAT GUITAR BACKS

GUITAR BACK

ONE PIECE
DULCIMER BACKS

MANDOLIN BACK

FIDDLE BACKS

This drawing shows how a hardwood log is entirely split (quartered) up for use in arched instruments, fiddles, arched mandolins, and guitars or cellos.

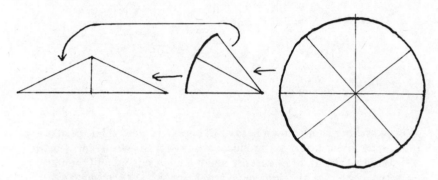

This last drawing shows how a hardwood log is completely milled up into stock for flat instruments.

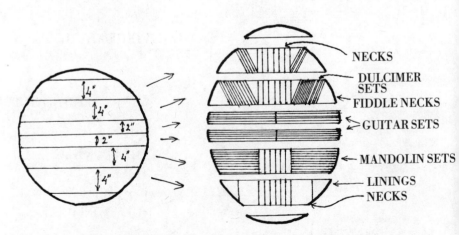

NECKS

DULCIMER SETS

FIDDLE NECKS

GUITAR SETS

MANDOLIN SETS

LININGS

NECKS

All of this stock will need to be air dried for about 3 to 6 years.

Aging Your Lumber

Once the lumber is cut to the desired stock size for aging, it must be sealed at the ends with wax so that it does not lose moisture too fast, causing it to check. This wood should be stored in layers with sticks in between. This allows the air to circulate around the wood. It is best to store the lumber in a cool dark place.

After the wood has aged this way for 2 to 5 years it can be cut up further on a band saw into matched instrument sets. Then the sets are stickered again and cured about another year before using them to make instruments.

BOOK MATCHED ROSEWOOD GUITAR BACK

Humidity

This subject could take up a whole book, but for our purposes I will try to keep it short. As the humidity rises, moisture is absorbed into the wood, which then swells and expands. As the humidity goes down, moisture is released from the wood, which then shrinks and contracts. It is best to build instruments when the humidity is low, at about 50%. 60 or 65% is too high. Check with your local weather bureau, but as a rule of thumb, it is good to build instruments when the weather is hot and dry or cold and freezing. It is bad to build instruments when the weather is hot and humid or cold and rainy.

Have fun building, and watch the weather.

TOOLS

The planes shown in the photograph above were hand made in my shop by a good friend. They are a fine example of what can be done with a few scraps of wood. These planes were made for about one dollar each (which is approximately the cost of the second hand blades at a junk store). All the other materials used were left over from other projects.

In this chapter, I want to introduce you to the tools used in making instruments. Most of these are common woodworkers tools that can be used for many other kinds of work. Some are special tools used only in instrument making. To help you to avoid the expense of purchasing new and costly tools, I will give some diagrams with instructions on the assembly of some tools that you will need, so that you can make your own.

Sharpening

Before delving into making the tools, I wish to explain sharpening. A knife, plane or other tool that is not sharpened properly is almost useless. Can you shave your arm with it? If you can't, it's too dull! This photograph shows my set-up for sharpening. From left to right are: my medium stone for rough sharpening; a white Arkansas stone for sharpening the edge; a soft Belgium stone for honing off the burr; and finally, a piece of board with two leather strips for stropping to razor sharpness. Also in this picture is a can of honing oil which is used with the stones. The oil reduces friction and prevents the stone from becoming glazed (the pores becoming clogged with metal). The Belgium stone is a water stone, so instead of using oil, you use water with this one. Finally in the picture is a package of razor stropping compound. This is used with the leather strops and acts to polish the edge to razor sharpness.

When using the stones, grind the blade around and around in a circular motion. Go gently, and use the whole surface of the stone. Use plently of oil and watch the angle of sharpening. The diagram below shows the way knife and plane blades are to be sharpened.

KNIFE

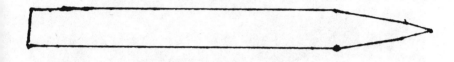

PLANE

The next diagram shows how a scraper is sharpened.

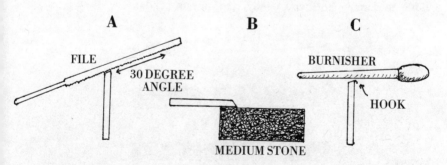

(A). The edge of the scraper is filed with a flat bastard file to a 30 degree angle. (B). Now the flat sides of the scraper are rubbed on a medium stone to remove the burr. (C). The edge is burnished—that is, pressed with a burnisher down the entire length of the scraper. This causes the sharp edge to fold over, making a hook. If you don't have a burnisher, you can use a screwdriver or other hard steel rod.

Fret Saw

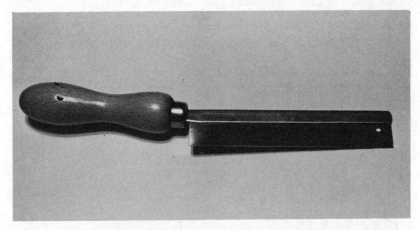

As I have stated elsewhere in this book, fret wire comes in different sizes. As you can see in this picture, the tang of the wire varies in width. Most back saws cut a slot too wide for the fret wire to fit into snugly, so you will need to grind the set of the saw. The set of the saw is shown in this diagram. The teeth, after being sharpened, are bent one left, one right, one left, one right and so on down the saw. This must now be ground down by rubbing the sides of the saw on a medium stone until the saw will cut a slot the right width for the fret wire being used. Keep testing your set as you grind. Do this by cutting slots in a piece of scrap wood and trying to fit the fret wire. When you get a snug fit and are not able to remove the wire easily, the saw is ready.

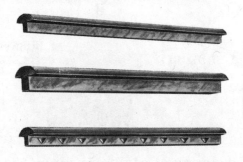

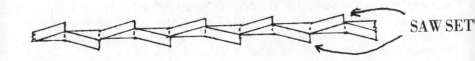

SAW SET

Tools

The following tools are some of the ones used in instrument making. These are outside calipers used for checking the thickness of faces, backs or sides.

These are violin makers' calipers for checking thickness in a changing surface.

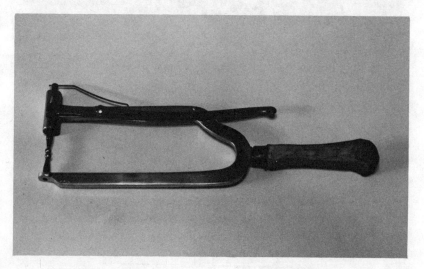

These are two scrapers; one is square, and the other has a slight curve to it.

This is a burnisher, used for forming the hook on a scraper.

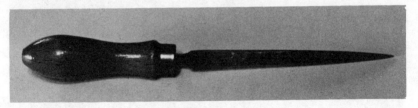

This diagram shows the different shapes of scrapers that can be bought or made from old saw blades.

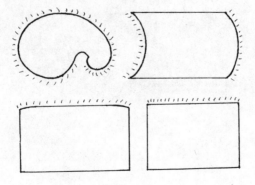

These are the knives I use in my shop. They are a large and a small skew knife, and a chip carving knife.

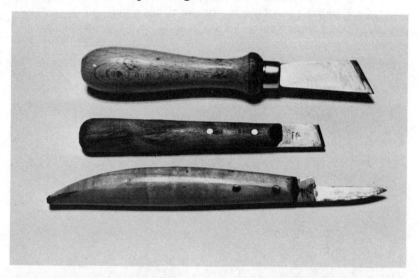

This is a curved bottom plane that I made. I use this in routing the inside of fiddle backs and bellies.

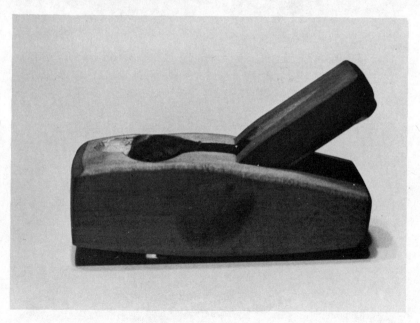

These two planes are most useful. The larger one is a smoothing plane used in the palm of your hand for leveling surfaces and truing small joints, and the small one is a finger plane, which you use between your thumb and index finger. It is very useful for many small jobs, such as doing linings, bindings, heads, edges, and much more. This little plane cost me about $3.00 and it is the one I use the most.

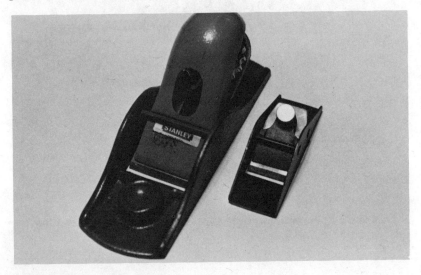

Special Tools
This is a deep throat clamp, used for clamping on guitar bridges.

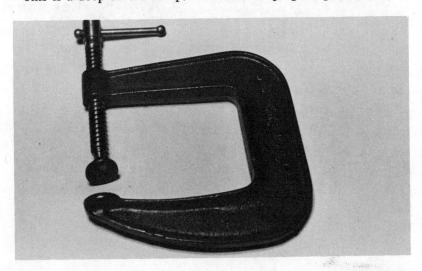

This is a purfling cutter. The guide next to the blade enables you to cut an even channel around the edge of an instrument for the purfling and binding.

This is a sound post setter. It is used as described in the chapter on fiddles.

These two tools are a reamer and a peg shaper. They are used for fitting friction pegs (wooden tuning pegs). The reamer makes a tapered hole, and the shaper makes a tapered peg.

Making Your Own Tools

In the rest of this chapter, you will find diagrams of tools that you can make for a fraction of what it would cost if you bought them.

Bending Iron

A SECTION OF CAR EXHAUST PIPE 8" LONG

B TWO HOLES DRILLED FOR MOUNTING HEATING ELEMENT

C 600 WATT HEATING ELEMENT

D PORCELAIN LIGHT SOCKET

E WASHER

F BRACKET FOR MOUNTING THE ELEMENT INTO PIPE

G BOLT FOR MOUNTING THE BRACKET

H HEX NUT FOR MOUNTING THE BRACKET

I WASHER

J NUT FOR MOUNTING ELEMENT ONTO BRACKET

K HEAVY DUTY ELECTRIC CORD (TOASTER CORD WILL DO)

L U BOLT FOR MOUNTING BENDING IRON ONTO HOLDING BOARD

M ASBESTOS OR SHEET ROCK 2" x 4" x ½" TO PREVENT BURNING THE HOLDING BOARD

PLYWOOD BOARD 8" x 5" x ¾" WITH 4

N HOLES DRILLED FOR U BOLTS

O U BOLT WASHERS

P 4 NUTS FOR U BOLTS

Exploded View

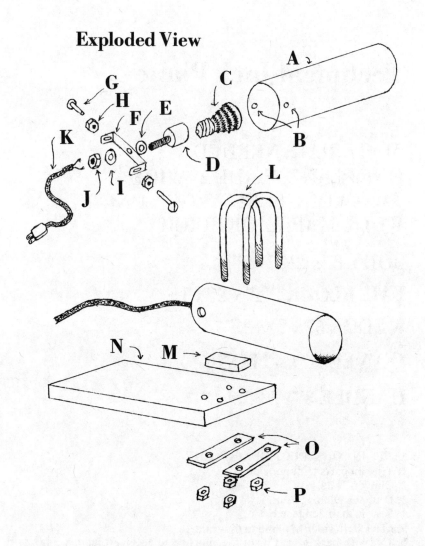

All you need do is to assemble this. You will control the heat by plugging and unplugging when necessary. If you have a vice you can clamp the bending iron in that eliminating the need for a holding board.

Technical Jack Plane

MATERIALS NEEDED
ONE PLANE BLADE 2" WIDE
TWO WOOD SCREWS 1¼" LONG
WOOD MAPLE, OR BIRCH

BODY 8" x 2½" x 2"

TAIL BLOCK 2½" x 2" x 1½"

WEDGE 5" x 2" x ¾"

DOWEL ¼" x 4" LONG

HANDLE 3" x 1½" x 1"

STEPS IN CONSTRUCTION OF PLANE
1. True all parts to dimensions
2. Glue on Tail Block
3. Drill dowel holes ¼ in.
4. Saw in half lengthwise
5. Mark both sides of plane to diagram
6. Cut with back saw. Chisel the mortice to receive blade, wedge and opening for shaving.
7. Using ¼" dowels glue body halves together, clamp till dry
8. Clean off all glue from inside of plane
9. Fit handle to front of plane, join with wood screws and carve to shape
10. Carve tail block to fit your palm comfortably
11. With plane blade in place, cut wedge and shape it till it is a perfect fit against blade and plane walls
12. Sand entire plane and finish with a light coat of gun stock oil
These plans can be adjusted so that you can make other planes. Round Bottom, Jointer, or Smothing Plane.

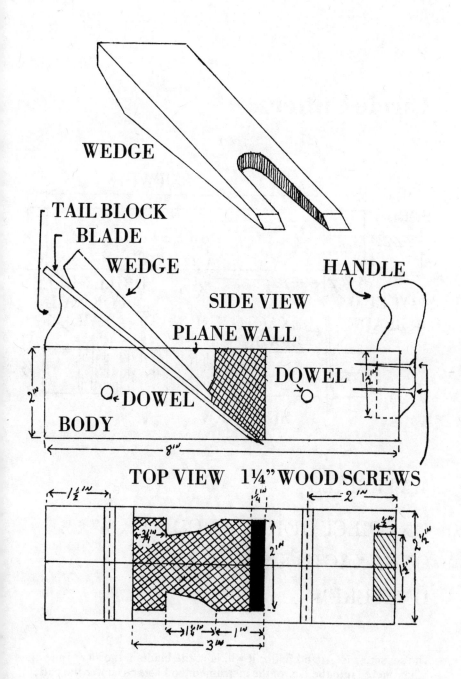

WEDGE

TAIL BLOCK
BLADE
WEDGE

HANDLE

SIDE VIEW
PLANE WALL

DOWEL
DOWEL

BODY

TOP VIEW 1¼" WOOD SCREWS

29

Circle Cutter

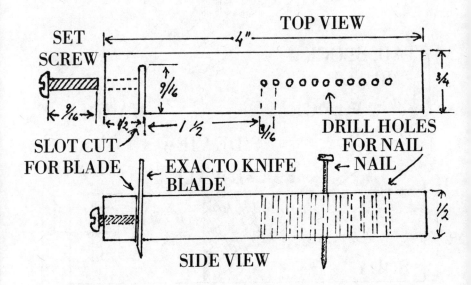

MATERIALS

ONE PIECE OF HARD WOOD 4" x ¾" x ½"

ONE EXACTO KNIFE BLADE

ONE SCREW

The set screw is ground flat so it will hold the blade in the slot. The nail is hammered into the face of the instrument and acts to center the cutter which is used like a compass, the diameter of the cut is decided by which hole is used.

Deep Throat Clamp

MATERIALS NEEDED

MAPLE 6½" x 3½" x 1"

DOWEL ¼" x 4"

ONE 3/8" SQUARE NUT

3/8" ALL THREAD 4" LONG

3/8" WING NUT

STEPS OF CONSTRUCTION

1. Cut out block of maple as shown in Fig. 1. The waste wood can be saved for a knife handle
2. Cut mortise slot ½ in. wide by 1 inch deep in pieces A and C. Then cut a tenon on both ends of piece B, as shown in Fig. 2
3. On piece A drill a 7/16 in. hole down through the end exactly ½ in. from end and center
4. On piece A fit the nut into a notch cut in the tongue and lightly glue it in place, using not so much glue as to get in the threading. Fig. 3 and 4.
5. Next join pieces A, B, and C as shown in Fig. 4 and glue, when glue is dry, make two ¼ inch holes in A and C all the way through and glue in dowels.
6. Have wing nut welded to all thread, then grind the end of all thread round and smooth
7. Round off tongue on piece C and sand entire clamp

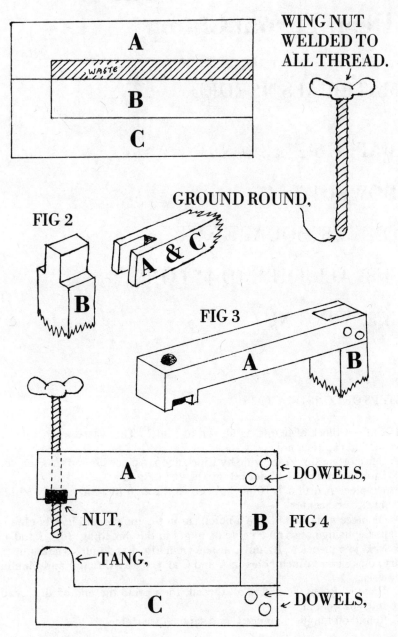

FIG 1

A

WASTE

B

C

WING NUT WELDED TO ALL THREAD.

GROUND ROUND,

FIG 2

A & C

B

FIG 3

A

B

A

DOWELS,

NUT,

B

FIG 4

TANG,

C

DOWELS,

32

Cutting Boards

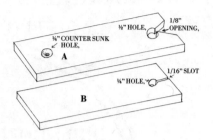

A. This board is used bolted to the work table for support when cutting with a coping saw. It measures about 6" x 3" x ½"

B. This board is used clamped to the work bench for cutting with a jeweler's saw. It measures about 6" x 3" x ½"

Calipers

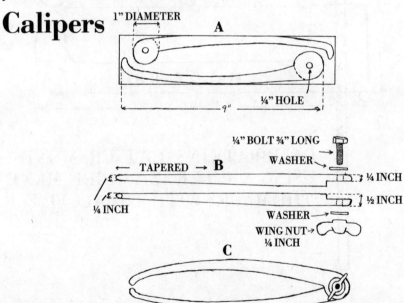

STEPS IN CONSTRUCTION OF CALIPERS

A.
A block of wood 2"x10"x½" is cut out as shown, drilled and sanded

B.
Exploded view of Calipers

C.
Assembled Calipers, the wing nut will set the opening

Fiddle Makers Calipers

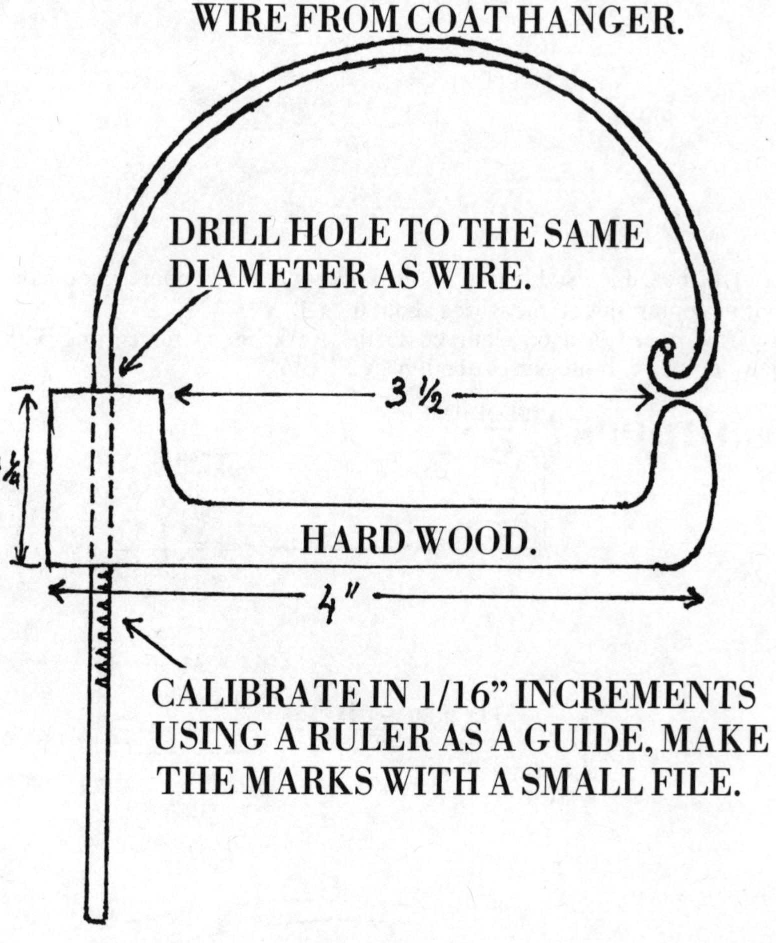

WIRE FROM COAT HANGER.

DRILL HOLE TO THE SAME
DIAMETER AS WIRE.

3 ½

1 ¼

HARD WOOD.

4 "

CALIBRATE IN 1/16" INCREMENTS
USING A RULER AS A GUIDE, MAKE
THE MARKS WITH A SMALL FILE.

STEPS IN CONSTRUCTION
1. Cut a section of coat hanger and bend it as shown
2. Take a block of hardwood measuring 4" x 1¼" x ½", and cut it as shown
3. Drill a hole in the wood and put the wire through. This must be a snug fit for the caliper to work
4. Now calibrate it in 1/16", starting from a closed position

BUILDING THE DULCIMER

The Dulcimer—A Short History and Other Points of Interest

The dulcimer is the first instrument discussed in my book for three reasons: (1.) it is the easiest instrument to build; (2.) it is the easiest instrument to play; (3.) this book is concerned with country and folk music and musical instruments, and the dulcimer is a folk instrument if there ever was one. A rock or jazz band would be an unlikely place to find a dulcimer player. However, country and folk music have a long and respected association with this instrument, and people who are interested in any aspect of this type of music are very likely to be familiar with the dulcimer.

DULCIMER MADE BY AUTHOR

As with most musical instruments, nobody knows much about the dulcimer's beginnings. In Scandinavia there are instruments that are probably the ancestors of the American dulcimer.

In this country, the dulcimer had its beginnings in the Appalachian Mountains, where people would sit out on their porches in the evenings after a hard day's work, and play a few tunes before turning in for the night. Ah ...... the sweet sound of a dulcimer singing out an old fiddle tune, or a haunting melody about a love gone wrong...... the sound entices you with its magic.

Incidentally, two good books on the playing of the dulcimer are: **In Search of the Wild Dulcimer** by Robert Force and Albert D'Ossche; and **The Dulcimer Book** by Jean Ritchie.

Dulcimers come in many shapes and sizes. The two most common are the tear drop shape and the hour glass shape. (See below.) Other common dulcimer shapes are the fiddle shape and the lute shape. I will show, step by step, how to build an elliptical dulcimer. I have chosen this, as it is the simplest one to make.

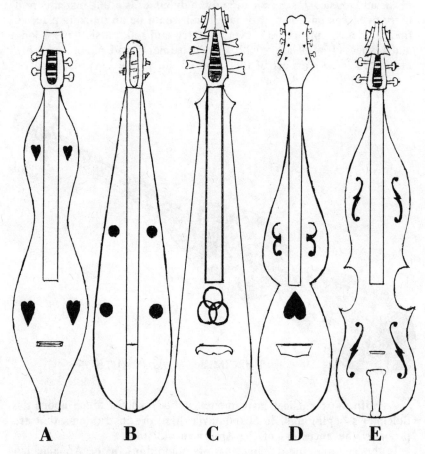

A **B** **C** **D** **E**

A HOUR GLASS
B ELIPTICAL
C LUTE SHAPE
D DOUBLE TEAR DROP
E FIDDLE SHAPE

36

Building the Form for the Dulcimer

Your first task is to assemble your materials. They will include: two (2) 1/4" dowel sticks; one (1) piece of pressed board or plywood (pressed wood is cheaper) measuring 3/4" by 32" by 8"; and four (4) pieces of the same material measuring 3/4" by 4" by 32".

Now take the latter four pieces, and glue them together, using two pieces for each side. Glue and clamp them and leave them to dry for six hours. If you don't have clamps available, you can nail them together until the glue is dried. Leave enough of the nail protruding so that it can be taken out when you are ready to put the sides together. You now have two board sandwiches for the sides of the dulcimer.

Next, using the template in the back of the book, cut a piece of cardboard to the shape of the dulcimer. Make sure that you do this with precision. Now cut your cardboard pattern to the final half shape of the dulcimer. Trace its outline once on each of the two sandwiches you have for the two sides. When this is done, cut along the traced outline with a band saw.

MARKED SIDES

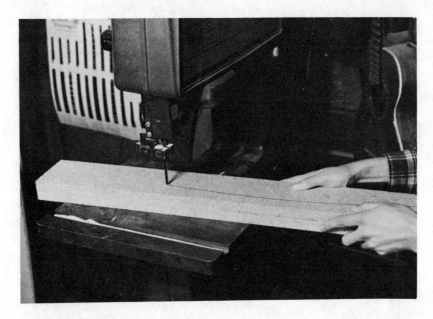

SAWING SIDES

It is worth your effort to do this job with a band saw, but if you do not have one, you can take the glued boards to a cabinet shop and have it done for you. It should not cost too much. It is important that this is done right because it will affect the final outline of the instrument you are building.

Next, take the board that measures 3/4" by 32" by 8" and draw a line completely down the center of the full length. This line will serve as a guide later on—a center line for building the instrument. It is also very important to keep this as the exact center of the instrument, so that everything else will line up properly.

Now, using your template sheet, trace the outline of the instrument onto this base board. When this is completed, you can glue your sides to that. Glue them in place and clamp them securely. Leave them for six hours to dry. Once again, if clamps are not available, the sides can be nailed to the base board with the nails protruding enough so that they can be removed after the glue is completely dry.

TRACING OUTLINE ON BASE OF MOLD

Next, you trace a line about 3/4" from the outside shape of the instrument, on the outside of the mold, all the way around. Then cut it to its final shape. The last thing left to do is to drill holes in the baseboard, about 1½" from one another, all the way around the edge.

SAWING OUT MOLD

MOLD SAWED OUT

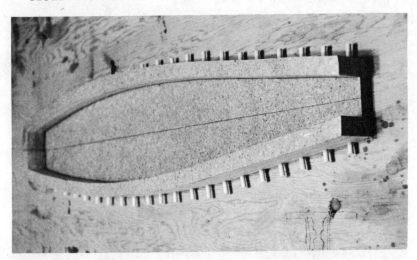

FINISHED MOLD

Next, take the two dowel sticks and cut them into one inch segments. Hammer these into the holes that have been drilled all around the sides. They will be used later for clamping on the top and back of the instrument. The mold is now finished except for a final sanding and cleaning up.

Gluing the Center Joint

If your wood is wide enough, you can cut the dulcimer top out of a single piece. But if you have no wood the width of the dulcimer, you will have to glue two pieces of wood together.

To make your glue joint, you need a jointer plane. If you don't have one, make a sanding stick. Use a very straight board or an iron bar three feet long. With contact cement, glue a strip of coarse sandpaper down the full length on one side.

Now. put your boards in a clamp with the two edges that will be joined facing up. Plane or sand those edges until they are completely level and true. Take the boards from the clamp, and rub the edges back and forth across the sandpaper until the fit between them is perfect.

Place the pieces on the work bench, with the edges that will form the glue joint fitted together. Clamp a board on one side, as shown. On the opposite side, hammer six nails into the work bench alongside the board. They should be evenly spaced, about 1/4'' away from the face board, and should protrude about 3/8'' from the work bench.

Now you will need to make six small wedges, as shown in the photo. Also get three bricks and two strips of newspaper.

JOINTING FACE OF DULCIMER

Place one strip of newspaper on the bench to prevent the glue joint from sticking to the bench. Apply glue to both board edges that will be joined. Lay them face down on the bench, fitting the center joint together.

Now, put the wedges on the bench between the nails and the side of the board. Push the wedges in slightly to apply pressure to the glue joint.

Lay the other strip of newspaper over the glue joint, and put the bricks on top of it to hold the joint down and keep it even. Hammer the wedges in tighter, and leave the face board to dry overnight.

It goes without saying that it will be easier if you have a wide enough board to start with—a board with a nice even grain. Then no glue joint will be necessary.

Planing the Top to Thickness

The top of the dulcimer should be about 3/32'' thick all over. Clamp your face board on the table face side up, and smooth down the whole face with a scraper and a block plane. When you've got it nice and smooth, lay your template on the board and lightly trace around it with a pencil.

PLANING THE FACE TO THICKNESS

Now, set your calipers at 3/32''. Turn the face over. Working on the back, plane and scrape the whole board, constantly checking the thickness to make sure you don't get it too thin. After you've got it down to 3/32'', sand it lightly all over with fine sandpaper.

Next, saw out the top with your coping saw. It's a good idea to cut it about 1/8'' outside of the line that you traced from the template, in order to give yourself a little extra wood to work with. (See photograph.)

Making the Fretboard

A blank of hardwood measuring 1/4'' by 1-1/4'' by 22-5/8'' must be planed smooth and flat. When this is done, use the template sheet in the back of the book and mark all the fret positions onto the fingerboard. Next, with a fine back saw, cut the fret slots. It is a wise idea to first test your saw on a piece of scrap wood. Saw a shallow slot and hammer in a piece of fret wire. If it does not fit snugly, you will need to file the set off the saw until you can get a snug fit. This process is shown in the chapter on tools. Once you are certain of your back saw, go ahead and carefully saw your fret positions just deep enough to allow the frets to be hammered home. After all the frets are in place, file the rough edges smooth.

HAMMERING FRET WIRE INTO SLOTS

Gluing on the Fretboard

The main thing you want to be sure of is that the fretboard is well centered on the face and that it is kept flat during the gluing operation. To do this, first lightly draw a line down the center of the face. Then center the fretboard on it perfectly. When you are satisfied that it is right, trace around it lightly with a pencil while holding it down and in place with your other hand. Then remove the fretboard. Next, get two pieces of wood measuring about 24" by 2" by 1". Be sure that these are perfectly true and flat. Apply glue to the bottom of the fretboard and lay it on the face where you have already marked its position. Now, using the two boards, one above the fretboard and one below the face, clamp it down tightly and leave it to dry overnight.

GLUING FRET BOARD TO FACE

Cutting the Sound Hole

Next the sound holes must be cut. This is done using a sharp knife or a coping saw. You can use a heart-shaped sound hole which is traditional, or an "F" hole which is used on a fiddle, or whatever you like. After this is done, you are ready to go on to bracing the face.

SOUND HOLES CUT WITH KNIFE

Bracing the Face

The diagram shows a bracing pattern that works well. Listed is the size of the braces.

"A," "B," and "C" cross braces measure 1/2" wide by 7/16" deep. "D" and "E" are muslin patches glued on to protect the sound holes. "F,""G," and "H" are the fan braces, 1/8" wide by 1/8" deep. "I" is the X brace, measuring 3/16" wide by 1/8" deep. "J" is the patch 1½" by 1½" by 1/16" thick.

GLUING ON BRACES

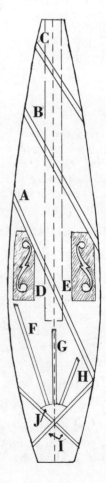

This photograph shows braces "A," "B," and "C" being glued in place. They are left to dry, and then with a chisel they are tapered off at the ends so that the ends will be 3/16" high.

Next you make the X brace ("I") by notching two pieces of wood into one another and gluing them in place. After that, the ends of the X brace are tapered down to nothing with a chisel. Now fit and glue the patch in place. After the glue is dry, glue on the fan braces "F," "G," and "H." When the glue on them has dried, they are tapered off to nothing at the ends as you did with the X brace. The last thing to do is to shape all the braces with a small plane to a rounded shape as shown in this diagram, and glue the muslin patches ("D" and "E") on the sound hole.

SHAPE OF BRACES

Preparing the Back

If you are using plywood for your back and sides, all you need to do is cut them out according to the template.

If you are using solid wood, make the back the same way you made the face. Brace it with three bars 1/2" wide by 3/8" high, as shown in diagram.

BRACING PATTERN FOR BACK

BRACING PATTERN FOR BACK

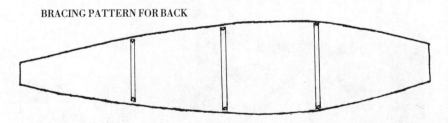

Sides

Plywood sides will need no planing. But if you are using solid wood sides, you must plane them to 3/32" thickness. Then cut the sides to measure 2" wide by 31" long.

Bending the Sides

When you are ready to bend the sides, first hold them under water for about 30 seconds to get them wet but not soaked.

Heat your bending iron. Take one side and bend it over the bending iron by rocking it back and forth. Keep rocking it, exerting gentle firm pressure, until it bends to the shape of the template. Do the same with the other side.

A word of caution here—if the iron begins to get too hot, unplug it and keep on working as it cools. Don't let the iron get so hot that the wood burns. A little scorching is normal and can be easily scraped off, but the wood must not be badly scorched. It's a good idea to practice first with a spare piece of wood until you get the feel of it.

After the sides are bent, place them in the mold. Wedge them in so that they will hold their shape.

Making the Lining

If you are using plywood, you can use the leftover strips for lining by cutting them into four strips 1/2'' wide by 29'' long. Bend them the same way you bent the sides. Then clamp them into the mold.

If you are using solid wood, you can make the lining out of any hard or soft wood. Saw your wood into four strips 1/2'' wide by 1/4'' thick by 29'' long. Make little saw cuts every quarter of an inch along the lining strips, sawing them almost all the way through. Or, bend them without cutting as you did with the sides, using the iron.

Making the End Blocks

You will need to make two blocks to fit into the ends. The back block is 1/2'' by 2'' by 2'', with one side cut to the same curve as the bottom of the instrument. Now cut the head block to the dimensions shown in the diagram.

HEAD CUT TO SHAPE

47

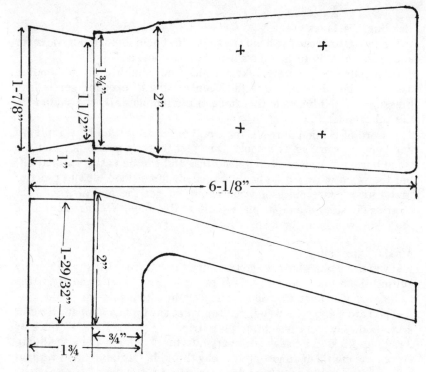

Assembly

Apply glue to the curved surface of the bottom block. Place it in position in the mold, and clamp it in place. Be sure the seam is closed tight. (See photograph.)

GLUING IN HEEL BLOCK

48

Next, fit the head block into position, and glue it in place in the mold. Clamp it. Leave the blocks to dry for several hours.

GLUING HEAD TO SIDES

Gluing in the Lining

The best clamps you can have for clamping the lining in place are clothes pins with rubber bands wrapped around them to give them extra clamping power.

Apply glue to a strip of lining. Fit it in place and clamp it on tight with the clothes pins. Do this on both sides. You will find that after you do this, the sides hold their shape very well.

GLUING ON LINING

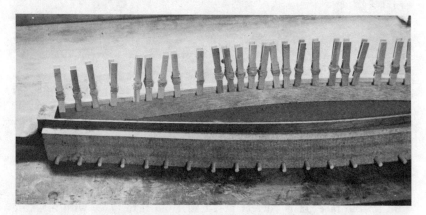

Now make a sanding board. Take a piece of plywood 3/4" by 8" by 16" and glue coarse sandpaper to the bottom of it. Rub the sanding board back and forth over the instrument until all sides and blocks of the dulcimer are perfectly level and smooth.

Gluing on the Back

Turn the dulcimer assembly face side down in the mold and wedge (with small sticks) the sides in place. Check to see that the back will fit easily in place on the sides with no gaps, and then remove the back and apply glue to the sides, head block and tail block. Replace the back on the dulcimer and tie it down tightly with rope, being careful to keep it centered.

GLUING ON BACK

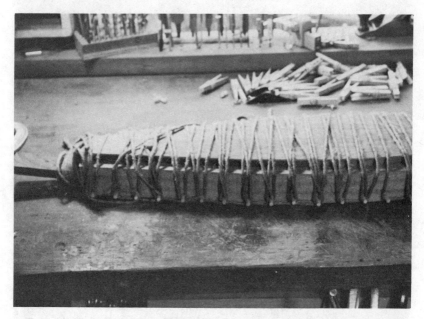

Let this dry overnight. When it is dry, remove the rope and use a small knife and plane to trim the edges. Now you can turn the dulcimer over in its mold so that it is back side down. If you want to, now is the time to put in a label. Place it on the inside of the back so that it can be seen through the sound hole.

Fitting the Face

Draw a center line on the end of the head block. Using that as a guide, line up the face in its correct position. Hold it in place with masking tape.

Now take a pencil and mark where the braces will tie in to the lining. Remove the face. Using a small saw or sharp knife, cut out notches in the lining to receive the braces. (See photograph.)

NOTCH CUT TO RECEIVE BRACES

When this is done, you are ready to glue the face onto the sides. Apply glue to the face, lining and sides. Place the face on the sides, fitting it into position. Working from one side to the other, tie the face down in place with the rope until it is held securely. Allow the glue to dry overnight. Then remove the dulcimer from the mold and check to make sure that all joints are solid and tight. Trim up the edges of the face with a knife and small plane as you did the back.

GLUING ON FACE

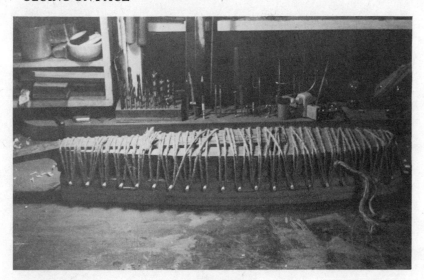

Making the Nut

Take a small piece of hardwood or bone and fit it in the channel you cut at the end of the finger board. After it is fitted, mark where you want the strings to go (an equal distance from one another except for the unison strings at left) and cut notches that the strings will ride in.

TUNING MACHINES AND NUT ARE FITTED IN PLACE

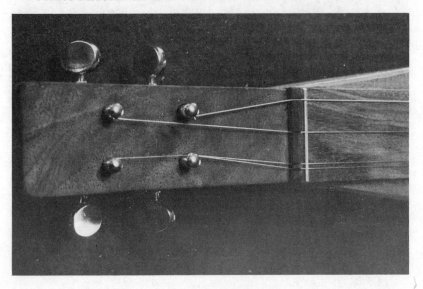

Fitting Tuners

Drill four holes in the head. The diameter of these are decided by the size of the shaft on your tuning machine, or the size of the bushings if they come with the tuners. The tuners will be held in place by small screws, but don't mount them until you have finished the instrument.

String Pins

These can be either guitar bridge pins (as shown in the photograph) or piano bridge pins. The guitar pins are fitted by drilling a hole (the same size as the shaft on the bridge pin) all the way through the tail block, and are used with ball end strings as shown in the diagram. Piano bridge pins are fitted by drilling a hole (the same diameter as the pin) into the tail block, and hammering them in place, as shown in the diagram. These can accommodate loop end or ball end strings.

BRIDGE, SADDLE AND PINS

USING
BRIDGE
PIN

USING
PIANO
PIN

String Saddle

The string saddle is a piece of bone (sold as a guitar bridge saddle) fitted into a groove cut in the end of the face. This will prevent the strings from pushing into the face wood.

Finishing

Sand your instrument all over. Start with sandpaper of 120 grit. Then go to the 220 grade, to the 400, and finally to the 600. When the dulcimer has been completely sanded, and all wood surfaces are smooth as silk, go to the chapter on finishing.

String Up

After the instrument is finished, all you need do is mount the tuning machines. For a bridge, you can use a banjo bridge which is so cheaply bought that it is not worth making. Set the bridge 27 inches from the nut, but don't glue it, as the string pressure will hold it in place fine.

Now string up your instrument and play. I have designed this dulcimer to that you can use either guitar or banjo strings; experiment with different gauge strings and tunings. I would suggest using two .010 plain strings, one .016 plain string, and one .023 bronze wound string. Try tuning it D-A-D or C-G-C.

FINISHED DULCIMER

BUILDING THE MANDOLIN

LUTE MANDOLINS

ARCHED TOP MANDOLIN

MANDOLIN LIKE INSTRUMENT. MADE FROM THE SHELL OF AN ARMADILLO

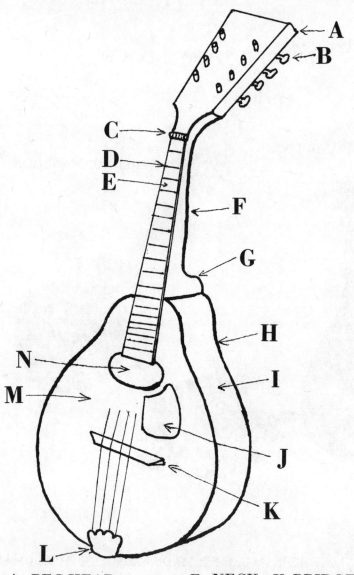

A	PEG HEAD	F	NECK	K	BRIDGE
B	TUNING MACHINE	G	HEEL	L	TAIL PIECE
C	NUT	H	BACK	M	FACE
D	FRET	I	SIDES	N	SOUND HOLE
E	FRET BOARD	J	PICK GUARD		

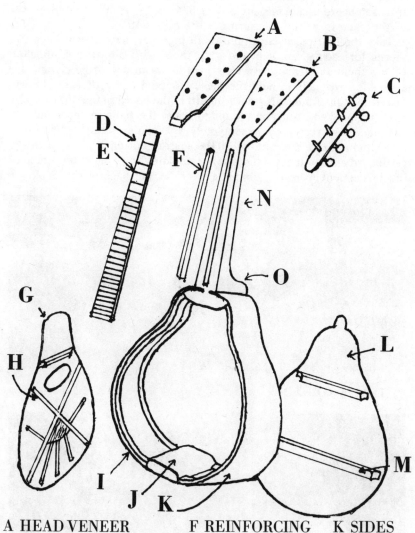

A HEAD VENEER   F REINFORCING   K SIDES
B HEAD   G FACE   L BACK
C TUNING MACHINE H BRACES   M BRACES
D FRET BOARD   I LININGS   N NECK
E FRETS   J TAIL BLOCK   O HEEL

Building the Form for the Mandolin

First assemble your materials. You will need the following: one (1) dowel stick, 1/4'' in diameter; one (1) piece of pressed board or plywood (pressed board is cheaper) measuring 3/4'' x 14'' x 20''; four (4) pieces of the same material measuring 3/4'' x 7'' x 15''.

Take the four pieces and glue them together, so that you have two pieces for each side. Join and glue them with aliphatic resin glue. Clamp them and leave them for six (6) hours to dry. If no clamps are available, use nails to hold the pieces together until the glue is dry. Leave enough of the nails protruding from the board so that they may be readily removed. You don't want to leave the nails in the mold.

When these sections are completely dry. you are ready to cut sides from them. Trace the outline of the instrument on a piece of heavy cardboard and cut it out. This is your template. You can get the shape of the instrument from the template sheet at the back of the book.

TRACING OUTLINE

TRACED OUTLINE

Placing the template on your two glued boards, one for each side, trace its outline on the boards. Remember to turn our pattern over so that you have a left side and right side. Now, using a band saw, cut the boards along the outline, following precisely the line that was drawn from the template.

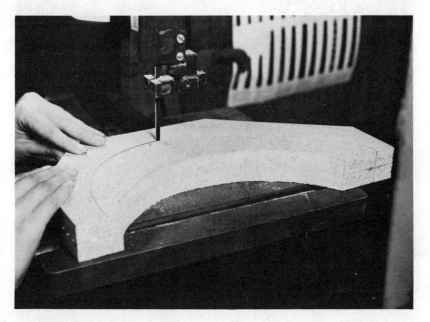

SAWING SIDES OF MOLD

It is important to do this with a band saw. If you don't have one available, it is worth spending the money to have the job done right at a cabinet maker's shop. Precision cutting is critically important for the success of the instrument you are building.

The next step is take your 3/4" x 14" x 20" board, and draw a line down the center the full length of the board (20"). With this line as a guide, mark off the inside shape of the instrument, using your template sheet to give you the correct shape.

You should have the bottom of the mandolin template about an inch from the bottom of the board. Now you will need to glue the sides to this board, using the lines drawn as a guide to show you where to glue the pieces. Be sure to glue them in the proper places, as this will affect the final outline of your instrument.

GLUING SIDES ON MOLD BASE

Next, mark a line about 1½'' from the center line above the form where the neck will be. Then mark another line, about 3/4'' outside of the instrument shape. Draw this line completely around the mold. Cut it out along this line, and your mold will be finished, made in the shape shown in the picture.

SAWING TO FINAL SHAPE

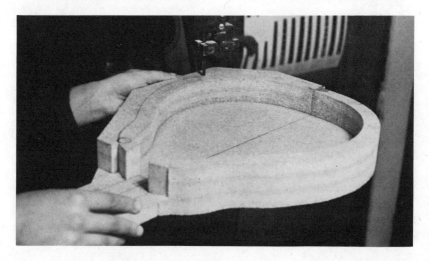

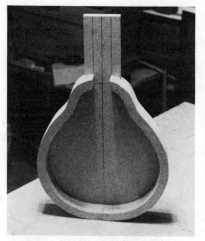

FINISHED MOLD

The last step in finishing the mold is to drill holes in the base board all the way around, about 1½'' away from one another. These holes should be drilled about 1/2'' deep into the base board. Next, cut your dowel stick into one inch (1'') pieces. Hammer and glue them into the drill holes, all around the mold. They will be used later for tying down the top and back when these have been glued on to the instrument.

At this point your mold is finished, except for a final sanding to clean it up. You can go on to build your instrument.

Making a Mandolin

I am giving instructions for making two different mandolins. One is the standard mandolin with floating bridge and tail piece. The other design has a pin bridge, which I happen to like better for tone. The floating bridge is easier to make.

Making the Neck

The neck can be made in either of two ways. You can make it out of a single block of wood measuring 3''x3''x16'', or you can build up the neck out of a board that would have to measure 1''x3''x22.''

If you make the neck by building it up, you have to stack the wood on top until you have 2'' of thickness where the heel is, as shown in the photo. Next you have to saw at an angle through the neck in order to develop the head. Cut this as shown in these photos. Then turn it around and clamp it to the neck as shown in the diagram. Plane the two surfaces of the angle cut until they match each other perfectly. Next, turn it around and glue it on. The photo shows a method of gluing which will enable you to keep everything lined up perfectly. This must be left to dry overnight in order to insure a good fit. Later there will be a lot of tension on this glue joint because there are eight strings coming off of the head.

GLUING UP HEEL

MARKED HEAD

CUT HEAD

TURNED AROUND

HEAD GLUING TO NECK

Your next step is to saw the slots for the sides to come into the neck. To do this you must find the exact place, according to the diagram, where the sides will fit into the neck. This line should be marked out with a square. Be sure to have the sides perfectly square to the neck.

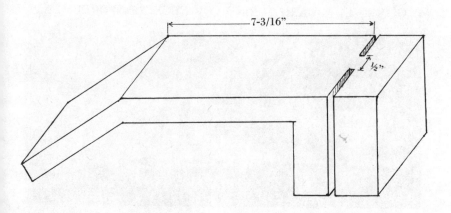

7-3/16"

½"

63

It is not necessary to reinforce the neck of a mandolin, but if you wish to reinforce it, you may. It can be reinforced with a piece of half-inch (1/2'') square tubing inlaid into the neck, running the full length of the neck. This is done by cutting out a channel one-half inch (1/2'') wide and one-half inch (1/2'') deep from the head down through the end of the neck. This channel is then inlaid with a piece of half-inch (1/2'') square tubing which you glue in place and leave to dry for a few hours. Later on, the fingerboard will be glued over that and it will make a solid neck. Guitar necks are reinforced by this method too.

Next, glue on the head veneer. This consists of a piece of veneer about one-eighth of an inch (1/8'') thick. This is done primarily for decorative purposes, but it also serves to strengthen the head.

HEAD VENEER GLUED ON

CHANNEL CUT

GLUING IN SQUARE TUBING FOR NECK REINFORCEMENT

Carving the Neck, Head and Heel

The first step is to draw a center pencil line down the full length of the neck and through the center of the head. Using this line as a guide, lay the template of the head design centered on the line, and trace around the template. Cut along the traced outline with a coping saw or band saw. This must be done very carefully. Keep the saw moving directly up and down at all times, so that you don't drift from the outline. After you have sawed off the waste wood, clean the head with scrapers and sandpaper until it is smooth and flush.

Next, start carving the heel. This is cut with knives and a chisel until it reaches its final shape. Go slowly on the heel. Make certain this carving is very smooth. A round heel is suitable for a mandolin, as shown. Then put the neck aside until later.

FINISHED NECK

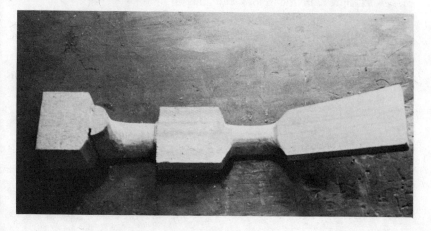

Making the Face

For your first step, take the two matched pieces of wood and join them down the center. Begin by planing the sides that are to be joined perfectly flat and true, until you can hold the sides together against the light without seeing any light coming through at the joint. This is best done with a jointer plane. If a jointer plane is not available, you can do it by gluing sandpaper to the side of a level or other absolutely straight object, and sanding back and forth across the two pieces of wood until they match perfectly.

**CUTTING TOP WITH
JOINTER PLANE**

Next, glue the two pieces together. Use a jig to hold them firmly in place until the glue dries. (This jig is demonstrated in the chapter on guitars, with instructions on how you can make the jig.) Or, glue the pieces as shown in the photo and diagram.

**GLUING CENTER JOINT WITH
NAILS AND WEDGES**

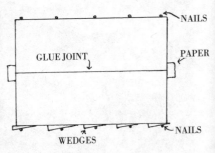

After the two pieces are perfectly glued together and the glue is completely dry, they can be taken from the jig. Now plane this section to the proper thickness, 3/32''. First plane the top of the board until it is perfectly flat and level. Then turn it over and work on the other side. At this point, check to make sure that you don't plane it thinner than 3/32''. It is all right to leave it slightly thicker, since some of the wood will be sanded off later during the finishing process.

PLANING TOP WITH SMOOTHING PLANE

CHECKING THICKNESS WITH CALIPERS

Next, trace the outline from the mandolin template sheet onto the face. Mark off where the sound hole will go. Trace the sound hole.

If you wish to inlay a rosette or any other decoration upon the face of your mandolin, this is the time to do it—before the sound hole is cut. So if you want to use a rosette, turn to the chapter on ornamentation and follow the instructions. It is not necessary to have a rosette or any other ornamentation around the sound hole. It's purely a matter of esthetics — something that's nice to have, if you like ornaments.

After the rosette is inlaid and sanded flush with the face, it is time to cut out the sound hole. The sound hole in a mandolin is oval rather than round. It cannot be cut out mechanically. It must be cut out by hand or with a deep throated coping saw. A good sharp knife will do the job. Go slowly around the hole with your knife, making just a slight cut as you go. Don't try to go completely through the face with one cut. It will take four or five successive cuts to clear away the wood. Take it easy. Go slowly and do a clean job, going around and around the hole until you finally cut through.

CUTTING OUT THE SOUND HOLE

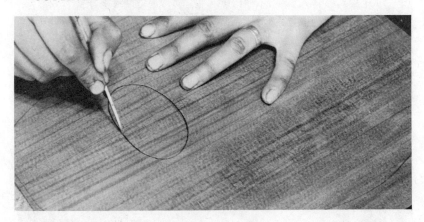

Now take the template and trace the outline of the mandolin onto the face. Saw it out to shape, using you coping saw or band saw.

SAWING FACE TO
SHAPE

The next step is putting on the bracing. This is probably the most important step in making a mandolin as far as tone is concerned. It is also critical for creating an instrument that will last for many years. So take the indicated stages very carefully, one by one, and get the job done right.

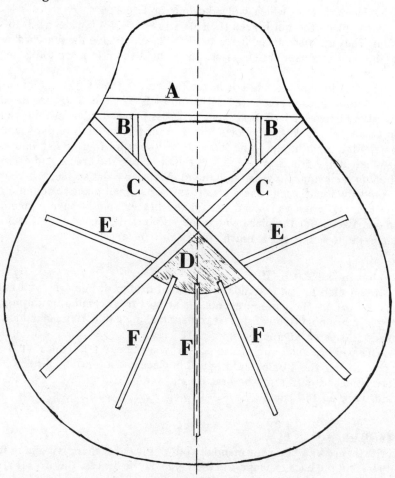

The braces in a mandolin include the main X brace (C), the fan braces (E) (F), the main cross brace (A), and the small braces (B) that go around the sound hole. The main cross brace (A) is 1/2'' wide by 3/8'' deep, and is equal to the width of the mandolin. The angles of the brace must be planed perfectly square. It is then glued in place with a very fine application of glue, clamped or wedged into position, and left to dry for three or four hours.

The X brace (C) is made of two pieces of wood 3/8" wide by 1/4" deep by 10½" long. The two braces are planed square and notched 4½" from the end, as shown in the diagram. Next, they are planed perfectly flat on the bottom and then placed on the mandolin face. Glue them to the face and use clamps or bricks to weight them in place until the glue is dry — which will take four or five hours.

Next, place the fan braces (E) (F). These are 1/4" wide by 3/16" high. They are also planed perfectly flat. Place and glue them according to the diagram, using bricks or clamps to hold them in place until they are dry.

The last braces you will put in are the braces (B) at the side of the sound hole. These braces are 1/4" wide by 3/8" high. They are fitted tightly in between the X brace and the cross brace. Take your time and fit these well, for they support quite a bit of tension around the sound hole. Glue them in place and leave them to dry for four or five hours.

When all the braces are dried, it is time to plane the braces and carve them to their final shape. Clamp the mandolin to a flat surface where it is held solidly in place. Use a small knife or a small plane to round off the braces. When you are done, all the braces should have a round shape. Except for the place where they tie into the sides, they should taper off to a flat clean finish, flush with the face.

Gluing in the Patch [D]

If you plan to use a standard mandolin bridge design, you will not need a patch. The patch prevents the strings from coming up through the face in a pin bridge design. If you are making a pin bridge mandolin, place the patch at this time.

The patch is made up of a piece of wood about 1/8" thick. It fits perfectly into the X brace and is glued in place and left to dry. When you have finished putting in the bracing and the patch, put the face aside and work on the back.

The Back

If you are building your mandolin out of plywood, there is nothing to do but cut the back to shape and then glue on the braces. But if your are making the instrument out of solid wood, with a two piece back, it will be necessary to join the two pieces that form the back.

It is traditional to insert a strip of inlay or purfling, or perhaps just a strip of plain wood, between the two pieces. However, this is not necessary. A good glued joint, if it is clean, will look perfectly all right.

The back pieces are joined in the same way that the face sections were joined. They are glued together in the same manner, unless you are using a center strip. If so, it should be inserted at the time of gluing.

Plane the back, as you did the face, to the specified thickness. For the back, the required thickness is 1/8'' instead of 3/32''. Do this with a plane and scraper until everything is perfectly smooth and flush.

Next, trace the outline of the mandolin from the template onto the back. Saw it to shape, using your coping saw. Then make a patch to go over the glued joint, to strengthen it. Make this of wood with the grain going in the direction **opposite** to the direction of the grain in the back. It can be made of a strip of wood left over from making the back. This is placed on the inside of the back, over the glued joint.

This strip should be about 1/2'' to 3/4'' wide. It runs the full length of the back. After it is glued in place over the glued joint, sand it and plane it until it is smooth all the way up and down.

The last step is gluing the braces. There are only two braces on the back of the mandolin. One goes just below the spot where the sound hole is on the face. The other runs across the back at the widest part. These braces are 1/2'' wide by 1/2'' deep by the width of the instrument. Glue them in place and weight them in position with bricks, or hold them with clamps, until the glue dries.

GLUING BRACES ON BACK

PLANING BRACES TO SHAPE

When the glue has dried, clamp the back to a table and plane the braces to a rounded shape. Then sand them smooth. They should taper off to nothing at the edges where they are fitted onto the mandolin sides. The back is now ready and can be put aside until later.

The Sides

If you are using plywood sides, the only thing left to do is to cut them to the proper dimensions and bend them. If you are using solid wood sides, they must be planed to the proper thickness, 3/32''. After this is done, trace the dimensions of the sides onto them and cut them to these dimensions.

DIMENSIONS OF SIDES

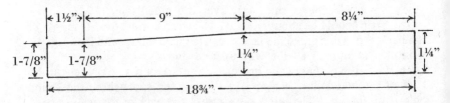

The next step is to bend the sides to the proper shape. For this operation, you use the bending iron that is described in the tool section. The bending iron must be clamped to the table or put in a vice, and left to warm up. While it is warming up, take the sides and hold them under the water for a couple of minutes — not long enough to soak them, just long enough to get them wet.

It's a good idea to have an extra side and practice on it first. Bending is really quite easy, but it takes a certain "feel" which you can only develop with practice. So take your practice piece of wood and after dampening it, rock it gently back and forth across the bending iron. You will notice that as you bend the side on the iron, the wood becomes like plastic when it reaches a certain temperature. Then you can bend it quite easily to the desired shape. The wood reaches the right temperature just before it begins to scorch. You have found the right point when your wood bends easily without scorching. You can only find this point by practice.

BENDING SIDES ON BENDING IRON

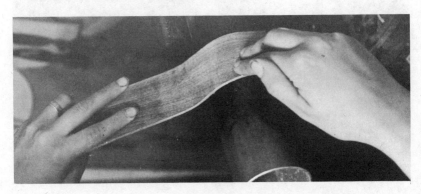

Once you've gotten the feel of it, take your sides and bend them to the shape of the manodlin, using your template as a guide. Make sure to bend them exactly to the shape of the mandolin template. Be careful not to scorch them. Some scorching usually does occur, but you must not scorch the sides so badly that you ruin them. A light surface scorching can be scraped off.

When you've gotten the shape you want, hold the side away from the iron. Continue to hold it in the desired shape until it has cooled slightly. Once it has cooled it will hold that shape.

BENT SIDES CLAMPED IN MOLD

After the sides have been bent and cooled, place them in the mold. Wedge or clamp them into place with sticks and leave them there for a day or so until they hold their shape firmly without support from the mold.

The next step is to glue the sides together at the bottom of the mandolin. This is done with a small heel block that measures 2" x 2" x 1". The two sides are glued at the bottom edge to meet this block half way. If you have used a center strip or purfling of any kind for the back, you will want to repeat this in the joint between the two sides at the bottom, so that the bottom will later line up precisely with the strip in the back. Leave the instrument to dry for four or five hours.

GLUING SIDES TOGETHER WITH HEEL BLOCK

When the glue has dried, you are ready to fit the sides, or upper bouts, into the neck. Make sure you have a good fit. The lining must be cut away where the sides fit into the neck. You should get a snug, but not tight, fit.

Before gluing, make sure that the instrument with the sides fitted into the neck will fit back into the mold comfortably. If it is too big to fit into the mold, that means the sides are too long and must be trimmed off just a little. Trim both sides equally, until the neck and body center comfortably into the mold.

When this has been accomplished, put glue into the slot and put the sides into that slot. Leave it to dry overnight.

The Linings

The linings provide a gluing surface to hold the back and face together. They are made of strips of wood the same length as the sides, measuring 1/2'' deep by 1/4'' thick. Bend them the same way you bent the sides, and into the same shape. Place the linings in the mold and wedge them in place with sticks until they are thoroughly cooled and dried.

You may wish to make a different kind of lining called a kerfed lining. For this lining, take a piece of wood the length of your sides, 1/2'' by 1/4'', and make little cuts every quarter inch along the entire length. These linings can be pushed into the sides without any bending, as they easily conform to the shape of the mandolin sides. I prefer a solid lining because it looks better and is quite a bit stronger in the long run.

Your next task is to glue the linings to the sides. You have already placed the sides in the mold, wedging them in place with sticks so that they take the shape of the mold. Now take a lining and glue it into place, along the edge of the side, clamping it into position by using clothes pins with rubber bands wrapped around them to give them extra clamping strength. You place these all around the lining, squeezing out excess glue as you go.

GLUING IN LININGS

After these are dry, you can take off the pegs and plane the edges perfectly square to the sides. When this done, the sides are turned over in the mold and the bottom edge is done with the lining the same way that the top edge was done.

LININGS ARE ALL GLUED IN PLACE AND LEVELED WITH SIDES

When this has been done, the sides are completely finished. You will notice that once the linings are glued to the sides, they hold their shape very well and they are quite a bit stronger than they were before.

Fitting the Face

The next step is fitting the top to the sides and neck. You do this by taping the top to the sides and neck which are still in the mold. On each side you have two braces that tie into the lining. Carefully mark the places where these braces meet the lining.

Now, take the top off, and cut notches in the lining (not in the sides— just in the lining) to receive these braces at the places you marked. When these braces fit into the notches very well, check the whole top and make sure that it lies nice and flat, flush with the whole mandolin.

When you have checked this out and you are satisfied that the fit is perfect, you are ready to glue on the top. Apply glue all around the edges of the face and top of the lining and in the notches. Position the face as you did when testing the fit. Tie it down against the sides, either with masking tape or light rope, and leave it to dry overnight.

GLUING ON TOP

The next day, remove the rope or tape and trip the edges with a knife so that they are flush with the sides. Sand them all around to get them smooth. Take the mandolin out of the mold, and clean up the inside joints with sandpaper.

Gluing on the Back of the Mandolin

Turn your mandolin over and put it in the mold face down. Check the line-up of the neck, making sure that it lines up perfectly with the center line of the mold.

When the back fits easily and smoothly all the way around, apply glue to the lining all around the edge. Also apply glue to the edge of the back. Put the back in place on the mandolin body. Tape it in position, or tie it with rope. Leave it to dry for four or five hours or perhaps overnight.

When it has dried, trim off the excess wood with a knife. Sand it smooth and flush with the sides. If you plan to put on a binding, now is the time to do it. Go to the chapter on ornamentation and you will find instructions on how to accomplish this.

Fretboard

Shape your fretboard by copying from the template. After it is cut to shape, plane the edges straight and smooth, and then plane it perfectly level.

Next, using the templete sheet as a guide, mark all the positions where the frets will lie. Next, cut all the slots. To do this, you will need a back saw which has had its set ground down on a sharpening stone to make it the right size saw for the tang of the fret wire being used. (This is described in detail in the chapter on tools.) Next, glue it in place. Be sure to line it up with the center line of the neck. Let it dry for five or six hours, then replane the fretboard so that it is perfectly level.

SAWING FRET SLOTS

GLUING ON FRET BOARD

FRET BOARD SANDED LEVEL. NOTE THE GROVE CUT IN END OF
FRET BOARD. THIS IS WHERE THE NUT WILL FIT.

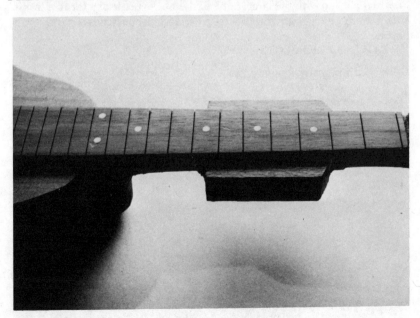

Cut the fret wire into the appropriate lengths and hammer it into place. Then use end snippers to snip off the ends of wire that protrude from the fingerboard. Use a long file to file the edges of all the frets flush with the fingerboard. Then at a 45° angle, the frets are smoothed down to the fingerboard so that there are no rough edges. Finally, sand all frets level and smooth to remove any filing marks. Now it is time to finish carving the neck. (Remember, part of the neck was left uncarved.)

First, carve the neck with a knife. Next work with a rasp, and then a file. Then scrape it into its final shape, being careful to keep it even and smooth all the way up and down. The surface should have the same feel all the way along the neck.

After this is completed, fit the nut in at the end of the fingerboard. This type of nut is made of bone and is filed to shape with a file.

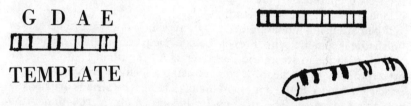

G D A E

TEMPLATE

Now the whole mandolin must be sanded from top to bottom. Every nook and cranny must be completely neat, smooth and clean. Begin with a medium sandpaper and go to finer and finer sandpapers until it is perfectly smooth all over and ready to take the finish.

Bridge

To make the bridge for a pin-bridge mandolin, you will need a block of wood measuring 4"x1¼"x1/4" thick. Cut this to shape as shown in the diagram. The slot is cut to accept the bridge saddle. This slot is 2" long by 1/8" wide and about 3/16" deep.

TEMPLATE

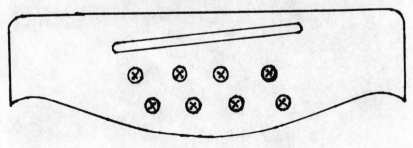

Now, if you plan to finish the mandolin with an oil finish, you should glue the bridge on before you apply the finish. But if you plan to use varnish, lacquer or French polish as a finish, the finish should go on before you glue the bridge in place.

To glue the bridge on, you will need two clamps deep enough to reach inside the instrument and clamp the bridge in place. Apply the glue both to the bottom of the bridge and to the wood surface on the spot where the bridge is to be glued.

If you have already put on a lacquer, varnish or French polish finish, trace the outline of the bridge onto the face of the mandolin. All wood where the glue joint will be made, between the face and the bridge, must be thoroughly scraped clean of finish so that the glue will hold. Be careful not to scrape off any finish past where the bridge will cover. When both the bridge bottom and the spot on the face that joins it are properly prepared and glue is applied to them, join them and clamp the bridge in place. Let it dry thoroughly.

If you are using a floating bridge, there is nothing more to do except finish the mandolin with French polish, lacquer, varnish, or oil.

Now it is time to string the instrument. All the tuning pegs must be fitted properly to the head. If you are using a floating bridge, you must attach a tail piece to the bottom of the mandolin. The strings are hooked into this tail piece. The floating bridge is simply placed under the strings and then positioned until the intonation is correct. The distance from the nut to the place where the bridge rests is 14.'' The nut must be notched as shown in the photo so that the strings lie comfortably in it. The notches should be filed deep enough so that the strings are low in relation to the fingerboard, and will rest on the first fret. Tune the mandolin and play awhile.

NUT AND TUNING MACHINES ARE FITTED

TAIL PIECE AND FLOATING BRIDGE

FINISHED MANDOLIN

81

BUILDING THE GUITAR

GUITARS MADE BY AUTHOR

Building a Form for a Guitar

Materials: You will need two (2) dowel sticks 1/4'' in diameter, and nine (9) pieces of pressed board or plywood. (Pressed board is cheaper.) The dimensions of these boards are: one (1) piece measuring 3/4'' by 30'' by 18'', and eight (8) pieces measuring 3/4'' by 21'' by 9''.

The first step is to glue together a sandwich for the side piece of the mold. This requires four pieces for each side. Use the pieces measuring

3/4'' by 21'' by 9''. Apply glue to both sides of the wood layers, and stack the layers in stacks of four. You now have two wood sandwiches with four pieces in each sandwich. After gluing them together, clamp them and leave them in the clamps until the glue is dry. If you are using aliphatic resin glue, it will be dry enough after about six hours.

If you have no clamps available, nail the boards together after gluing. Leave the nails sticking out so that you can easily remove them when the glue is dry.

Next, make a template for your guitar form out of thick cardboard. Copy it from the template sheet in the back of the book. When the board sandwiches are dry, lay the cardboard template on one of the sandwiches and trace an outline all around it, leaving an inch on either side at the end. Now turn your template over, and repeat the operation on the other sandwich. This gives you a right side and a left side.

TRACING THE OUTLINE ON SIDE

The next step should be done with a band saw. If you don't have a band saw, take the job to a cabinet maker's shop where it can be done for about a dollar. It is worth spending the money to have it done properly with a band saw, because an accurate mold is crucial to the shape of the instrument. If this is not cut right, the instrument will not be shaped right.

CUTTING THE SIDE

But suppose you have a band saw and are doing it yourself. Saw very carefully along the line that you have drawn, on the inside only. Try to make this cut in one clean sweep with no rough sections. Now do the same thing to the other sandwich, and that will give you the two sides of the guitar mold.

Next, take the larger board (the one that measures 3/4" by 30" by 18") and draw a line down the center, going the long way. This line must be exactly in the center because it will be a very important guide line later. Now lay your template sheet on the board and trace an outline of the guitar shape, starting with the bottom of the guitar about an inch away from the end of the board. This placement means that there is quite a bit of board left over where the neck will be.

TRACING THE OUTLINE ON MOLD BASE

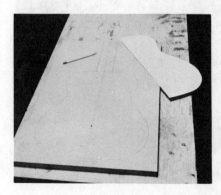
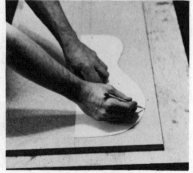

OUTLINE TRACED

After the outline of the guitar has been traced on the board, glue the sandwiches (the sides) to the board so that they line up exactly on the template outline that you traced. It is usually easier to glue one side at a time.

GLUING ONE SIDE TO BASE

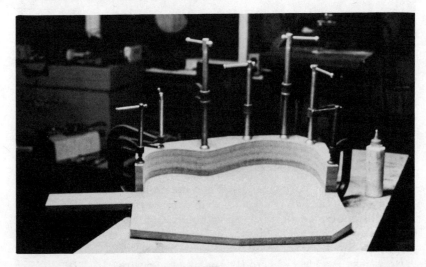

GLUING OTHER SIDE TO BASE

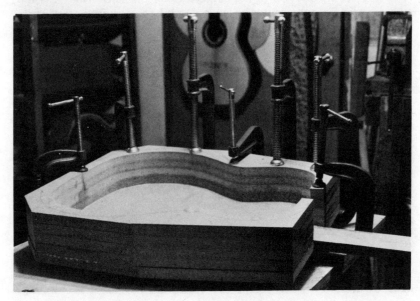

When the sides are glued in place and the glue is dry, draw a line around the outside of the guitar shape about 3/4" from the inside edge which has been cut on the band saw. You have already drawn your center line the length of the base board where the neck will be. Now draw two more lines, each about an inch out from this center line. This gives you a place to clamp the neck later on when you're making the guitar.

SAWING OUT MOLD

The next step is to cut precisely along the lines you have drawn. You now have your mold for the guitar. All you have to do is sand it and place the pegs around the bottom edge. To place the pegs, first drill holes all around the bottom of the base board about 1¼" apart. Cut the dowel sticks into 1¼" sections, and drive them into these holes. They should protrude about 3/4". You will use them later when you clamp the bottom and top of the guitar to the sides. When this is done, your mold is complete and you can go on to build your guitar.

READY FOR LAST STEP   FINISHED MOLD

Building the Guitar

The first thing to remember about making a guitar is that the whole operation must be completely planned out ahead of time before you even touch a piece of wood. For that reason, it is best to read through the entire section on guitar building before you start to work. That way, you'll have in mind exactly what you want to do and precisely how you want your guitar to look when it's finished.

When you are ready to start, the first step is to make the neck. The neck can be made from a solid block of wood measuring 4'' by 4'' by 24''. It can also be built from a block of wood measuring 1'' by 3'' by 36'' and built up in blocks into the shape of a head, as shown in the diagram.

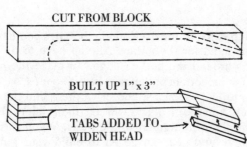

CUT FROM BLOCK

BUILT UP 1" x 3"

TABS ADDED TO → WIDEN HEAD

88

After the heel block is completely built up, glued together and allowed to dry, you are ready to build the head. This is done by sawing a slot as shown in the diagram. It must be sawed all the way through with a back saw. Use a back saw because it makes a clean cut all the way down that will be easier to clean up later.

After the saw cut is made, turn the piece of wood around as shown in the diagram, and clamp it to the rest of the neck. Use a plane or sanding blocks. These must be made perfectly level and smooth as shown in the diagram. The wood should be turned around again, and then glued in place. The photograph shows the gluing and clamping methods that insure getting the head glued on properly and smoothly.

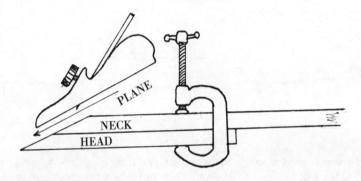

GLUING HEAD TO NECK

Leave the head to dry overnight. After the glue is dry, sand the top of the head completely level. Check it with a ruler to make certain that it is perfectly flat.

Usually at this point a piece of head veneer is glued on. This is a thin piece of wood, about 1/8" thick, that completely covers the area you have just glued.

After this is completed, check your measurements. Measure 15" from the head; this should bring you to the spot where the heel is connected.

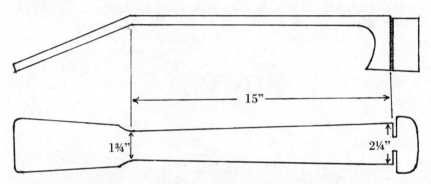

Now you need to make two slots, one on either side of the neck. Later the sides will fit into these slots. They must be very true and square to the face of the neck. So mark them off with a T-square. After they are marked off, saw down to within a half inch of the center line on each side of the neck. The slots should be sawed 3/32" thick if you are using solid sides, and 1/8" thick if you are using plywood sides.

The next step is the reinforcing of the neck. The best material for this purpose is 1/2" square tubing. This material is very strong and is commonly used on well-made guitars. I like it better than a truss rod because it does not put unusual strain on the neck, and it remains solid and straight for the life of the guitar.

NECK WITH CHANNEL CUT FOR REINFORCING

To reinforce with tubing, you must carve a channel 1/2" wide and 1/2" deep down the center of the neck, beneath the place where the fingerboard will go later. This channel must be made with very close tolerances. It can be done with a chisel, but it is much easier to do it with a power router if you can get one.

When the channel is cut, see if the square tubing fits into it exactly. You should have a good snug fit. It should be tight enough so that you have to exert a little pressure to insert the tubing, but you should not have to force it in.

If the fit is correct, take the tubing out and apply either white glue or epoxy glue—just a little—all along the channel. Press your tubing into position, clamp it down tight, and leave it overnight to set. It should be flush with the top of the neck when you have finished.

The next step is to carve the head. Draw a line down the center of the neck and on down the center of the head. Lay your head template on the head and trace it. Using a coping saw or band saw, carefully cut along the tracing. Do as clean a job as you possibly can. If you are using a coping saw, be sure that it is perfectly square to the side. The cut can be cleaned up later with a small plane and scrapers, and then sanded.

Now you go to the other end of the neck, and carve the heel, as shown in the drawing. There are two basic types of heels. One is the round heel. It is the simplest to make. It can be carved with a knife and then finished with sandpaper, starting with a coarse grade and proceeding to finer sandpapers. The other is the pointed heel, which I prefer for its appearance. It's purely an esthetic choice. It doesn't matter which you use. The guitar will be equally strong with either. When you make the heel, be sure to bring it as close to the final dimensions as possible.

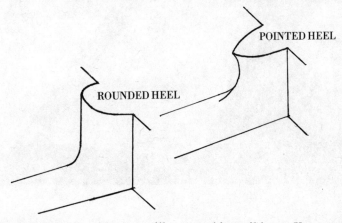

POINTED HEEL

ROUNDED HEEL

Now lay the neck aside; you will not need it until later, Your next task it to make the top or face of the guitar.

TOP

Joining the Top

The guitar top is made of two pieces of wood measuring 8'' wide by 20'' long by about 1/4'' thick or less. You will join them together lengthwise. Note that the little lines that make up the grain of the wood are closer together on one side of the board than on the other. The boards are joined on the sides with the closer grain. The pieces should be book matched, if you have a matched set of wood. If not, match them as best you can. Try to match the joint perfectly with the grain, so that you will end up with the joint as invisible as possible.

The best way to make this joint is with a jointer plane, as shown in the photograph. Lay the board on top of another board with the face in between and have both boards clamped solidly to the table. You can then run the plane on its side along the side of the face, so that you get a clean cut all the way along.

CUTTING TOP WITH JOINTER PLANE

You can check this joint by holding the two boards together with a light behind them. If you cannot see light between the boards, the joint is good. If you see any light through the crack, you must plane it again until the joint is perfectly light-proof.

If you have no jointer plane, you can get the same effect by taking the side of a level and gluing sandpaper to it. Rub it back and forth across the edge of the board until you get a perfect joint. This method takes quite a bit longer but works just as well. A jointer plane is best, but most people don't have one. If you plan to continue making instruments, or if you plan to do any cabinet of carpentry work, a jointer plane is a very good investment.

Next you glue the two top pieces together. To do this, you need to make a jig. For the jig, you need one board measuring 2'' by 3'' by about 20'' long, and five (5) pieces of wood measuring 1'' by 1'' by 18''. Nail the five pieces at equal intervals onto the larger board. Hammer the nails in far enough below the surface of the wood so that the nail heads won't mar the top. Then make some small wedges, as shown in the photograph.

GLUING JIG

The next step is to apply glue to the two edges that are to be joined. It's a good idea to rub a little wax on the jig over the point where the boards will be joined, so that they don't stick to the jig after the glue is dry. If you have no wax, place a piece of paper where the joint will be, to prevent it from sticking to the jig.

Now, with the boards in place on the jig, the edges of the sides glued and matched, start with a piece of rope at the end strut going across, and wrap it in a figure 8 pattern three or four times on each strut until you have completely tied the face together at all points.

TOP IS NOW TIED TO JIG AND WEDGES ARE PUT IN ONE AT A TIME TO ADD PRESSURE TO THE GLUE JOINT

After this is completed, take the wedges and squeeze them in between the ropes, so that they go under the cross in the figure 8 of the rope. Just tap them gently into place with a hammer. This exerts plenty of pressure on the face to force the glue joints together and, at the same time, keeps the face flat against the struts on the jig.

TOP LEFT IN JIG TO DRY

At this point, check the whole glue joint on top and underneath to make certain that it is perfectly lined up. While the glue is still wet, if there are places where the joint does not line up as well as it should, you can push the boards back and forth with your fingers until it all lines up perfectly. Now lay it aside and let it dry for several hours.

When the glue is dry, first remove the wedges and then untie the rope. Take the face from the jig and hang it up or lean it against a wall. Let it air dry overnight.

The next step is to plane the face to the right thickness. The finished thickness of the face is 3/32''. Plane one side with a small block plane until it is perfectly flat. Then turn it over and plane the other side, being careful not to go past 3/32'' thickness. Keep checking the thickness as you go along. It is better to leave it slightly thicker than 3/32'' because you will sand away some thickness in the final sanding of the guitar. But it must on no account be **thinner** than 3/32''. It is also important to get the thickness exactly even all over the guitar.

PLANING TOP WITH SMOOTHING PLANE

CHECKING THICKNESS WITH CALIPERS

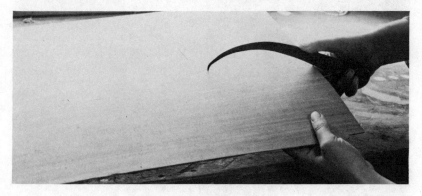

When the planing is completed, lay your template on top of the face and trace the outline of the guitar, using the glue joint as the center line of the face to center the template precisely. Mark a spot at the exact center of the sound hole. That will be important later.

TOP MARKED, OUTLINE AND CENTER OF SOUND HOLE

If you are planning to put a rosette or any decoration around the sound hole, do it now before you cut the sound hole. If you decide to do this, turn to the chaper on inlay and ornamentation and follow the directions for inlaying a rosette.

CUTTING SOUND HOLE AND PURFLING GROVE WITH CIRCLE CUTTER

Cutting the Sound Hole

In the chapter on tools you will find a design for a sound hole cutter. This cutter is simple to make and works fairly well. More expensive and elaborate ones can be bought.

CLEANING OUT PURFLING CHANNEL WITH NARROW CHISEL. THIS CHISEL WAS MADE FOR THIS JOB

When you start to use your sound hole cutter, you will notice that there are holes drilled in it at intervals. These permit you to cut different sized holes. Put a nail in the hole that will give you the right diameter for the hole you want in your guitar. Hammer this nail down into the face of the guitar and into the table below the face. Now, starting lightly, go around and around, making the cut a little bit deeper with each pass. Do not try to cut the hole out in one pass or you will tear the wood.

When the plug of wood that you have cut comes loose and is ready for removal, simply lift up on the sound hole cutter and the plug will come out with it, leaving a clean sound hole which can be sanded smooth. Now with your coping saw, cut the face to the outline you have marked.

CUTTING FACE TO SHAPE

FACE IS READY FOR BRACING

Bracing the Face of the Guitar

The next step is to brace the face of the guitar. This, in my opinion, is one of the most important operations. Your skill at this point will be the most crucial factor in the tone of the finished guitar. So take this part of the guitar building very seriously, and do each step as perfectly as you can.

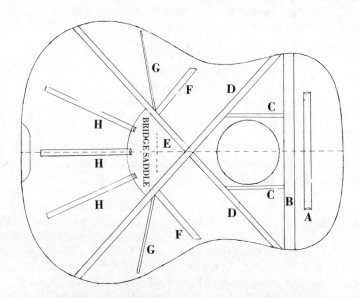

GLUING ON "B" BRACE

Beginning on the inside of the face, mark out lightly with a pencil and ruler where all the braces will go. Then, using very straight grained spruce or cedar, cut your braces to their basic shapes.

The X brace is the main brace. It will need to be notched and glued together before it is glued to the face. Cut it out and make the joint as shown in the diagram. Next, plane the bottom of the X brace so that it is perfectly flat. Now you are ready to glue it on. Apply glue very lightly all along the bottom of the X brace (none on the guitar), and place the brace in position over the pencil marks. Then clamp it in place. If you don't have clamps, weight it with bricks to hold it in place and apply pressure while the glue is drying. Leave it to dry for at least an hour.

When the glue is dry, the next step is to glue on the patch. When the guitar is finished, the patch will be under the bridge, where the strings come through. The patch prevents the strings from coming back through the soft wood of the face, so it should be made of a piece of hard wood. Perhaps you have a piece of hard wood left over from making the back. Scrap wood will do, providing that it is hard wood. It should be about 1/8'' thick.

Cut the patch to the shape it must be to fit snugly into the X brace. Take another piece of wood about an inch thick and cut it to the same shape as the patch. Apply glue to the bottom of the patch and push it into place between the X braces. Now, take your one inch thick piece of wood, put it on top of the patch, and weight the whole thing into place with a brick or clamp it. Leave it to dry for about an hour.

Next comes the cross brace which goes above the sound hole. This brace should be cut perfectly square. Then glue it to the face as shown in the diagram. Again you can weight it with bricks and leave it to dry for about an hour.

Now there is a smaller brace that you must position just above the cross brace. It helps prevent the face from contracting and expanding with changes in humidity, and helps prevent cracking around the fingerboard. You glue this on the same way you glued on the main cross brace.

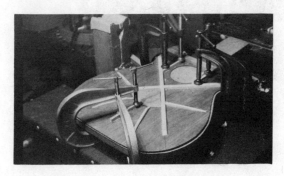

GLUING BRACES
ON FACE

Next, one by one, put on all of the fan braces and the braces that come from the side of the X's and go out toward the waist of the guitar.

After all the braces are glued in position, they must be carved to shape. See the diagram for illustration of the desired shape. You must get the braces smooth and round. Except for the tie-in braces (which tie into the guitar later), all the braces must be trimmed and tapered, so that they finally taper off flush with the face. When this is done, the face can be put aside until later.

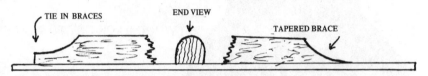

THIS IS HOW TIE IN BRACES ARE CUT AT THE ENDS

THIS IS HOW BRACES TAPER OFF

The back

If you are using plywood, making the back is a very simple operation. All you have to do is cut the back to the shape of the guitar, using your template, and glue on the braces.

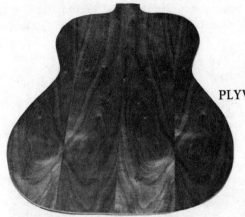

PLYWOOD BACK CUT TO SHAPE

If you are using solid wood, two pieces must by joined down the center, as the face was joined. Most guitar backs are glued with a center piece in between the two sections. This center piece can be either a strip of purling or veneer. It is used for the sake of apperance, as it gives a contrast to the two side sections. It is not necessary to use this strip. A good clean glue joint will do just as well.

WALNUT BACK WITH PURFLING STRIPS IN CENTER

Next, the back must be planed to the right thickness. Like the face, the back is 3/32'' thick in most guitars. I personally find, however, that if you leave the back 1/8'' thick or even a little thicker, it really seems to help the tone. Many people would disagree with me on this point, but that's my opinion.

After the back is planed to the desired thickness, the next step is to secure the center joint by putting a patch the full length of the guitar right over the center glue joint. This patch can be made of scrap wood left over from the back. However, the grain of the patch must run at right angles to the grain of the back. After the patch is glued in place and allowed to dry, plane it into a round shape and sand it smooth.

The next step is to glue the braces in the back. There are four braces in the back of the guitar. They go the full width of the guitar from one side to the other, and they are positioned at equal distances apart from one another. They include one in the upper bout, one at the waist, and two in the lower bout. They measure 1/2'' wide by 3/4'' high by the width of the part of the guitar where they are placed.

Cut the braces and glue them in just as you glued the braces of the guitar face. Then plane them round and even with a small hand plane and finish them with sandpaper until they are smooth to the touch. The back is now finished. You can put it aside and go on to the next step.

The Sides

If you are using plywood sides, all you have to do is to cut the sides to the proper dimensions and bend them into shape as described in this chapter.

However, if you are making sides of solid wood, there is an additional step you must take before you are ready for the bending. First, the wood must be planed to 3/32'' thickness. The sides must be 3/32'' thick throughout their entire length and breadth. Do this with scrapers and a small plane. Finish the wood by sanding it smooth with sandpaper.

Next, measure the sides to the exact dimensions that they must be for the guitar. Mark with a pencil, then cut them to their final shape with your saw.

DIMENSIONS OF SIDES

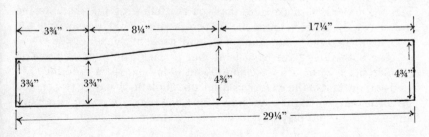

Now you are ready to bend the sides. This is the stage that most people worry about, although it is actually easy, once you learn to find the bending point. The wood bends readily when it reaches a certain temperature. But it takes practice to know when that point is reached, for if the wood gets only a little hotter than the bending point, it will scorch. It's a good idea to have a spare side or some scrap wood to practice on until you get the feel of it.

BENDING THE SIDES ON BENDING IRON

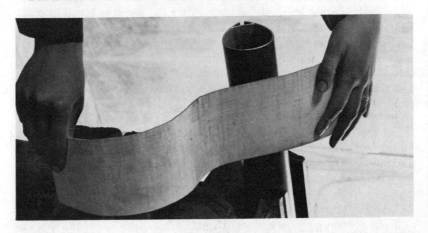

This is how you do it. Using the bending iron I have described in the section on tools, plug it in and let it warm up. While it is warming up, take your side and dip it in cool water for a moment or two, just long enough to get it wet. **Do not soak it.** Sides don't need to be soaked.

Now take the side to your warmed-up bending iron. Gently rock the part of the side you want to bend back and forth on the iron. At a certain point, you will feel the wood begin to give under gentle pressure. When it has heated up to just the right temperature, it will bend like a piece of rubber. Be careful not to force the wood around the iron, and not to let it heat up past the bending point so that it scorches. You should be able to bend the wood with very little scorching. Plywood sides bend very easily and are no problem at all. Use your template all through the bending process to make sure that you are following the shape of the guitar exactly. After bending the side on the iron, hold it away from the iron, until it cools a little and will hold its bent shape.

After both sides have been bent, put them in the mold and wedge them in place with sticks or clamps. This is to hold them until they are cold and the last of the water has dried out of them. A day or two should be sufficient. When they are dry, scrape and sand the sides to remove any scorching that may have occured. Get them completely clean. Be sure that they are thoroughly dry. Check them now to see how well they line up with the template. They must line up as perfectly as possible in order to make a guitar with the least possible stress in it.

BENT SIDES CLAMPED IN MOLD AND LEFT TO DRY

The next step is to bend the linings—or, if you are going to use kerfed linings, they must be cut. Kerfed linings work very well and are the easiest to insert. To make a kerfed lining, take a strip of wood 1/2" wide by 1/4" deep and about 30" long. Saw cuts in it at 1/4" intervals, not quite cutting through the strip. You will wind up with a strip as shown in the photograph.

MAKING A KERFED LINING

I prefer a solid lining myself. A good wood to use for solid linings is willow, as it bends very well. So does bass wood. Cut strips 1/2'' by 1/4'' by 30'' and bend them on the bending iron the same way you bent the sides, to the exact same shape. Leave them to dry in the mold for a day or two. When they are dry, glue them to the sides all around, using clothes pins with rubber bands tied around them for clamps. You must get a very close fit, with no gaps between the linings and the sides. The clothes pins squeeze all the glue out. This is done in the mold, to help keep the shape of the sides.

GLUING IN THE LINING

When this is completed, the sides will hold their shape very easily in the mold. The next step is to glue the sides together. Start by gluing in the heel block—the block that goes at the bottom of the guitar. The block measures 4¼'' by 1'' by about 3'' wide. It can be made of a scrap of wood left over from the neck. Glue the two sides to the block, making them fit perfectly to one another so that there is no gap left between.

At this point, if you have used a center line or purfling down the back of the guitar, you should repeat this in the joint between the two sides at the bottom of the guitar, as shown in the photograph. If you are just using one strip of purfling, the slot can be sawed out, after the glue has dried, and that piece inserted. Or you can insert it at the time of gluing.

Gluing the block may be done with your sections either in or out of the mold. I find it easier to do it out of the mold, so that I won't have a problem with glue dripping over into the mold. You will need several clamps.

GLUING TOGETHER THE SIDES WITH HEEL BLOCK

The next step is to fit the sides to the neck. This is very critical and has to be done properly. Be sure you have the sides marked as to what's the top and what's the bottom. And don't get the neck in upside down. This may sound funny, but I did it once and it is pretty maddening! If you get it in upside down, you have to take it apart and start all over again.

Check the fit of the sides into the neck. The fit must be snug. It should take a little pressure to force the sides into the neck.

After you have put the sides into the neck, check to make sure the whole guitar fits back into the mold. If it doesn't fit, then a small piece of wood must be removed from the end of the upper bout until you get a perfect fit with the neck at dead center. Once the fit is absolutely perfect, separate the neck and sides and apply glue to the inside of the neck (the part of the neck that will be inside the body). There is no need to put glue into the slot itself.

Now glue the sides to the neck. One or two clamps may be helpful, but they are not necessary if you have a good fit. Do this whole operation with the guitar in the mold to assure a good tight fit for the neck.

Use one long stick from the heel block to the end of the inside of the neck, to maintain the pressure against the sides. Let this dry overnight. After it is dry, you can take the guitar out of the mold and it should be relatively stable.

Fitting the Top to the Sides and Neck

Now you are ready to join the guitar face to the sides. The first step is to tape the face in place with masking tape. Now mark the four places where the braces that fit into the lining meet the lining. Mark these places clearly on the linings.

Next, remove the face. Carve out small notches in the lining where you made the marks—NOT in the sides, but only in the linings. These notches should by about 1/4" deep and about 1/4" wide. (They should be the width of the brace.)

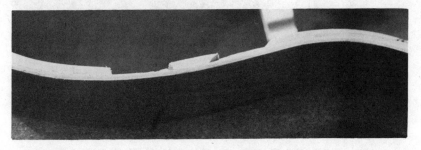

LINING NOTCHED TO RECEIVE TIE IN BRACES

Put the face back on the sides and see that the braces fit properly into the notches. When the face makes good contact with the notches, check all around to make sure that there is firm contact between the sides and the face at every point. Sand the surfaces with a flat stick wrapped in sandpaper until the fit completely satisfies you. You must get a very tight joint all around. The idea is to get it so that the face will sit on the top, right against the edges of the sides, with absolutely no pressure.

Now, remove the top. Apply glue all around the edge of the guitar face and around the top edges of the sides. Apply glue also at the points where the face goes over the neck block and where it goes over the heel of the guitar.

Put the face back in place so that all glued surfaces meet. Now tape or tie the face to the sides of the guitar inside the mold. Pull the tape or rope tight all the way around, until all glue is squeezed out of the sides. Leave it to set for at least four or five hours until you are sure the face is securely glued to the sides.

When the glue is completely dry, take your guitar out of the mold and check it all over to make sure that you got a good glued joint. Clean up any spilled glue. Sand around the inside edge of the top. Put the guitar back in the mold, face up, and trim all edges carefully. Carefully sand them smooth, so that the guitar can be taken from the mold and put back face down with no binding or snagging.

GLUING ON TOP

Now make sure that the guitar, placed face down in the mold, lines up perfectly so that the center line of the neck meets the center line of the mold, and the point where the sides are glued together at the bottom also coincides with the center joint of the mold.

At this point, you have the guitar face down in the mold and you have everything lined up just right. You are ready to fit the back onto the instrument. Place the back on the sides and make marks where the bracings meet the lining. Remove the back, and carve notches into the linings where the braces will come in. Now fit the back on, with the braces going into the notches, and make sure that it fits snugly all around. Make any adjustments necessary to insure that the back fits the sides as well as the face did.

When you have a perfect fit, you are ready to glue the back onto the guitar. Apply glue all around the edge of the back and the edge of the lining, where the two will meet. Spread the glue evenly. Now press the back into place on the sides. Tape it or tie it down and leave it to dry for five or more hours.

When the glue is thoroughly dry, trim all edges and sand them smooth. Take the guitar out of the mold.

Now your guitar is almost finished. You must be very careful from here on not to dent it or mark it.

If you have decided to use a binding on your guitar, this is the time to put it on. To apply a binding, turn to the chapter on ornamentation and inlay and follow the instructions there. If you are not using a binding, go ahead to the next step—putting on the fretboard.

Fretboard

Now you are almost finished with your guitar, and it is time for the final operations.

Cut the fretboard to the shape shown in the template sheet. Then trim the edges with a small plane so that it is smooth and clean all the way around. Make sure the top and bottom of the fretboard are planed very smooth, so that you can get a good glue joint between the surface of the neck and the fingerboard.

Now put the fingerboard exactly where it will go on the guitar, checking with the diagram for guidance. Line it up. Use your straight edge and be sure to get it perfectly aligned. This will insure that your bridge is in the right place.

Next glue the fingerboard in position, using clamps to hold it firm. Leave it to dry overnight. When it's dry, plane the fretboard completely level all up and down the length to remove any mark left from clamping it, and to bring it into proper alignment with the body. This is best done with a jointer plane, but can also be done with a shorter jack plane. If you use a jack plane, be sure to check your work with a straight edge.

GLUING ON FRET BOARD

PLANING FRET BOARD LEVEL

When you have done this, take your template sheet and mark off where all the frets will go.

A word or two on frets: Fret wire comes in different widths, as far as the tang is concerned—that is, the tang that goes down into the fret slot. Take a small back saw, the tool you will use for sawing the fret slots, and make a test cut on some scrap wood. Try hammering a bit of fret wire into the test cut. It should hammer in easily, make a snug fit, and not be easy to pull out again. It shouldn't be too stiff, though.

Most commercial back saws have the set a little too wide for this operation. You may need to grind off part of the set on a sharpening stone. You do this by moving the saw back and forth across the sharpening stone. Keep checking it to see when you can make a cut in your test piece of wood and have the fret stick just as you want it to when you hammer it in.

When you have your back saw adjusted to make the right cuts, saw slots for the frets to go into in the places you previously marked from the template sheet.

When doing this it is a good idea to tape heavy cardboard over the face to prevent it from becoming damaged with a slip of the saw or other tool. Hammer all the frets into the slots, and snip them off with a wire snipper at the very edge, as shown. Next you will file the sides of the fingerboard. At this point, be sure to put three or four layers of masking tape over the guitar body, near the edge of the fingerboard, so that the file does not scratch the body.

SAWING THE FRET SLOTS, NOTE HOW THIN PLYWOOD IS TAPED TO THE FACE TO PROTECT IT.

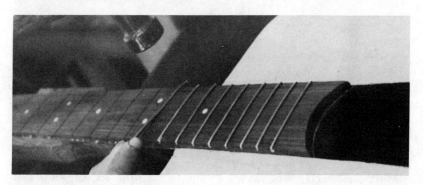

HAMMERING IN THE FRET WIRE

CUTTING OF EXCESS FRET WIRE

Carefully file the edges of the fretboard so that the frets are flush with the fretboard. Then, holding the file at a 45 degree angle, file all edges of frets until they make a 45 degree angle, from the edge of the fretboard to the top of the frets.

The next step is to file the whole fretboard so that all frets are level with one another. You do this by taking a 12" flat metal file and running it up and down the fingerboard until all the frets show at least some markings from the file. That means that since the file is absolutely flat, the frets, if they all show markings, must have become flat too. File lengthwise, not across. By filing lengthwise, you keep the frets prefectly aligned with one another.

Now you need to round the frets. You do this with a fret file. If you don't have a fret file, wrap a piece of sandpaper around your finger and run your finger up and down the board until all the frets are smoothly rounded off. They should feel smooth to the touch when you run your hand along the fingerboard, with no sharp edges.

When you have them all rounded and smooth, go to a fine 400 wet and dry sandpaper. Go over all the frets with this sandpaper and a bit of horning oil until all file and sandpaper marks are removed. When the frets are polished to their original smoothness, they will be perfectly level.

At this point, only the head and heel are carved. Now you need to finish carving the neck. Shave off all remaining edges. Shape the neck carefully, first with a knife or a small plane. As you begin to get it to the desired shape, go to a rather sharp rasp to cut it down to the right shape faster. Be sure to keep it even up and down the length, so that the curve of the neck is the same all the way up and down. Next, with a half round bask file (using the flat side) go over the whole thing again to smooth it. Finally go over it with a scraper until it is very smooth.

Then, where the carving of the heel ends and the neck starts, carefully bleed that in with a knife so that the sections blend very well together. You don't want an abrupt change from the carving of the heel to the carving of the neck. Do the same where the head joins the neck, so that all of it looks smooth and natural.

Now sand the whole neck and then the rest of the guitar very carefully. Go over the entire instrument from top to bottom, leaving no scratches or rough spots. Always sand in the direction of the grain. After sanding it all over with medium sandpaper, go to a very fine sandpaper. Go over it all again to remove the tiny scratches left by the medium sandpaper. This takes some time, so be patient. The longer you take at this stage, the better the final job will be. You wind up in the end with the finest sandpaper you can get, delicately polishing the whole guitar with it.

While you are doing this, be careful to keep your hands clean. Have a good safe place handy to put the guitar down when you're not working on it. Keep it as clean as possible. Now you are ready to finish the guitar. You have only one job left to do—making the bridge. If you are planning to use an oil finish, you must glue the bridge on before applying the finish. If you are using a lacquer, varnish or French polish finish, the bridge goes on after the finish is applied.

Making the Bridge

To make the bridge, you will need a block of wood 6'' by 1½'' by 1/4''. Rosewood or ebony is best, although you can use other good hardwoods. Turn to your bridge diagram, and carve the bridge to shape as shown in the diagram. Drill two holes, one at each end of where the bridge saddle will go. Cut a slot between them. This slot should be 1/16'' wide and it must be right between the two drill holes. You can carve it with a small knife or a very small, narrow chisel, if you have a chisel small enough.

Now measure the distance from the nut to the place where the bridge will be. The saddle should rest 25½'' from the nut.

Next, on the high E string side, add 1/8'' to that distance. On the low E string side, add 1/4'' to that distance. This should bring your bridge into perfect alignment.

With your bridge set at the right distance from the nut, you need to line it up perfectly with the fingerboard. Using a straight edge as a guide, get the bridge positioned so that the strings will come exactly down the center of the bridge. When you have found the right placement for the bridge, mark the place with a light pencil, and mark all around the bridge. Make the pencil mark **very** light, because you want to rub it off afterwards.

Now remove the bridge. If you have already finished the guitar with lacquer, French polish or varnish, you have to remove that finish from the spot where the bridge will be glued on. So very carefully, with a knife, trim all around the inside of the pencil markings, and scrape away all finish material within that mark. Scrape it down to the wood. The glue will not take on a varnished surface.

Next, position your bridge in the spot where it is to be glued. You've already drilled two holes where the bridge saddle goes. Now drill through these holes clear down into the guitar face. You can use these holes by putting small nails through the bridge and face to assure good alignment when gluing the bridge. When this has been done, apply glue to the under side of the bridge and a little glue lightly to the face, and glue the bridge in place. Next take a deep throat clamp and clamp the bridge to the face. Make sure you distribute pressure evenly over the whole bridge. Tighten the clamp to the point where a little glue is squeezed out all around the bridge. Leave the glue joint to dry overnight to assure a good set. Guitar bridges are likely to come loose from time to time, so it's necessary to have a good glued joint to start with.

GLUING THE BRIDGE

After the bridge is quite dry, take the deep throat clamps off, and mark the differences between all the pins in the saddle. Use the diagram in the book to show you where to make these marks. Drill holes for the pins. The pins should be a snug fit. They should come within 1/8'' of going all the way down into the holes.

DRILLING HOLES FOR BRIDGE PINS

BRIDGE PINS AND SADDLE ARE FITTED

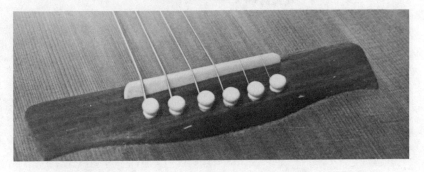

There is one last thing to do—fitting the nut at the end of the fingerboard. This nut is made of a piece of bone. Fit it in place and mark it with a pencil, so that it comes out just over the fingerboard, as shown in the photograph. Now, still following the diagram, mark off the distances between the strings, and notch the nut just lightly, so that the strings will ride over it.

NUT IS FITTED INTO GROVE CUT IN THE END OF THE FRET BOARD

Fit all tuning pegs to the head of the guitar so they they turn smoothly, and screw them down to the guitar.

THE TUNING MACHINES ARE FITTED

Setting the Action

For this step, you will need to string your guitar. It's a good idea to start out with a set of light gauge strings. Put them on the guitar and tune them almost up to pitch. Then file the nut with a small needle file, so that all the strings sit easily down into the nut, but not so far down that they brush against the wood and buzz. Do this a little at a time, checking frequently to make sure that you get a good fit, with the string not too high off the fingerboard but not too close.

When this is done, check the action at the bridge to see whether it is too high. The height of the bridge is set by filing the bottom of the bridge saddle until it sits in the right place. You should end up with the high E string about 3/32'' from the 12th fret. The low base string should be about 1/8'' from the 12th fret. You may either need to file the bridge saddle underneath to lower it, or, if it needs to be raised (which I doubt will be the case) you can shim it.

Now your guitar is finished. you are ready to enjoy playing it.

COMPLETED GUITAR

BUILDING THE FIDDLE

CARVED FIDDLE HEAD

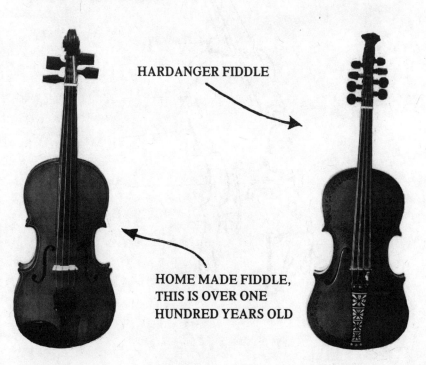

HARDANGER FIDDLE

HOME MADE FIDDLE,
THIS IS OVER ONE
HUNDRED YEARS OLD

A SCROLL
B EYE
C VOLOUTE
D PEG BOX CHANNEL
E TUNING PEGS
F NUT

G FINGER BOARD
H NECK
I HEEL BUTTON
J BACK
K UPPER BOUT (SIDE)
L BELLY

M "C" CENTER BO
N BRIDGE
O "F" HOLE
P TAIL PIECE
Q LOWER BOUT
R CHIN REST
S SADDLE
T END PIN

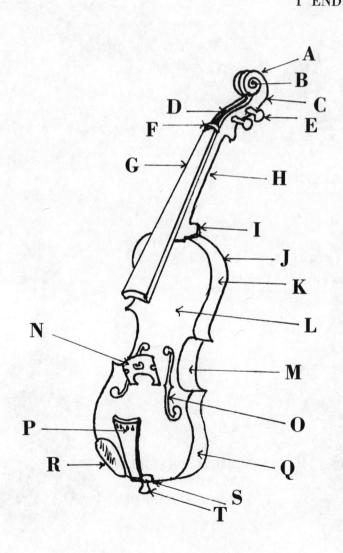

A BELLY   F LININGS   J BUTTON
B BASS BAR   G SOUND POST   K GLUE JOINT
C NECK MORTICE   H BOTTOM BLOCK L LABLE
D HEAD BLOCK   I BACK
E CORNER BLOCK

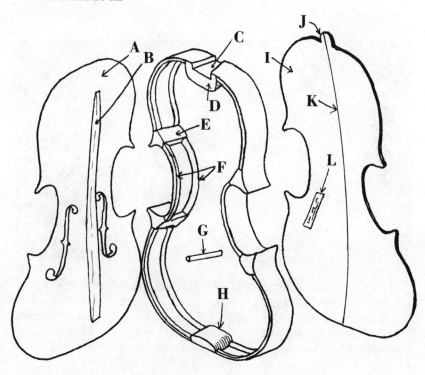

Building the Form for a Fiddle

You will need two molds during the construction of a fiddle. They have to be build separately. We will number them mold No. 1 and mold No. 2.

Mold No. 1

For this you need two boards. One must be 3/4'' x 11'' x 15''. The other measures 1/2'' x 11'' x 15''. These can be of pressed wood or plywood.

Stack one board on top of the other, and draw a center line down the middle. Make a cardboard template from the template sheet in the back of the book. Put this cardboard template on the board. Trace around it, thus tracing the outline of the mold onto the board.

TRACING OUTLINE

Next you work on the corner blocks. The locations of the corner blocks and the head and heel blocks must be marked off. The easiest way to do this is to punch holes in your cardboard template all along any lines and holes that must be drilled. Push pins clear through the template sheet into the wood. You will use the pin marks as a guide to drawing it out on the mold.

MARKING WITH PIN

MARKS LEFT BY PIN

MARKING CORNER BLOCKS

MARKING DRILL HOLES

When you have thus marked the places where the corners will be cut out, and where the head and heel blocks will be cut out, the next step is to mark all drill holes marked "A." Then mark all drill holes marked "B," and finally all drill holes marked "C."

MARKED MOLD IS CLAMPED

Now, with three or four small clamps, clamp the two boards together firmly so that they can't be separated. You must drill holes, countersunk, in the places marked "A." These holes should be wide enough to accommodate the head and the nut of a bolt. Now drill holes directly down the center of the countersunk spots. The holes should be a little larger than the diameter of the bolts to be used to bolt the mold together. The bolts should be 1¼" long and 1/8" in diameter, with nuts to match them.

HOLES ARE DRILLED FOR BOLT HEADS AND NUTS

NUT IS PUT ONTO BOLT

NOW THE NUT IS DRIVEN INTO THE MOLD BY HAMMERING ON THE BOLT

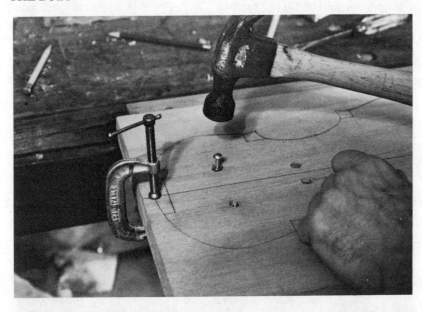

THE BOLT IS NOW REMOVED LEAVING THE NUT INBEDDED IN THE MOLD

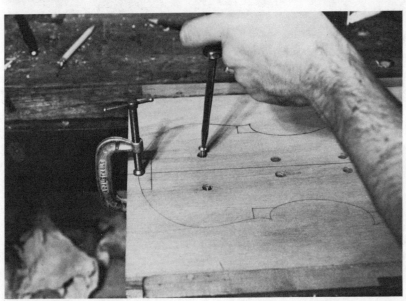

After all "A" holes have been countersunk and drilled through, countersink on the other side so that there will be a place for the head. Now drive the bolts through the holes so that the head is countersunk on one side, and put the nut on the other side. These bolts will hold the mold together until the time comes to take it apart. They will also enable you to take the mold apart easily then.

THE MOLD IS NOW TURNED OVER, AND THE BOLT IS DRIVEN THROUGH TO THE NUT

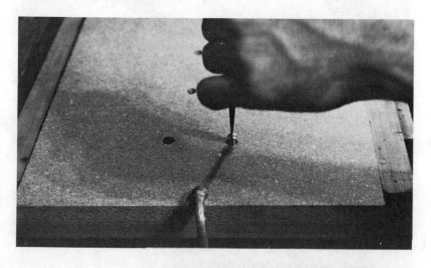

THE MOLD IS NOW HELD TOGETHER BY COUNTER SUNK BOLTS

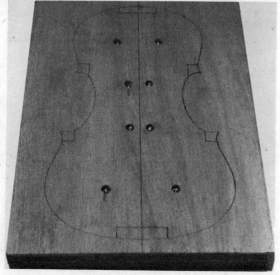

Now drill all the holes marked "B." They should be drilled rather large. You will use them for clamping the sides and the blocks into position. They are there simply to provide a place for the clamps to go in the mold. They should be about 1" to 1¼" in diameter.

USING A PUSH PIN TO MARK ALL OTHER DRILL HOLES

DRILLING LARGE HOLES WITH SPADE DRILL BIT

Next, drill the holes marked "C." They should be about 1/4" in diameter, drilled all the way through. They are on the corner where the blocks go, and are there so that later, when you are ready to cut the sides of the fiddle off the mold, you can easily get a saw or knife in there.

Now saw the mold to the shape as shown. Cut out the corner blocks and the head block.

MOLD IS READY FOR SAWING

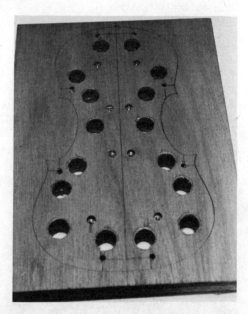

SAWING MOLD TO FINAL SHAPE

The next step is to dismantle the mold. On the bottom section of the mold (the piece that is 1/2" thick), drill eleven (11) holes at the spots marked "D." Drill these with a drill bit 3/32" in diameter. Then with a metal cutting tap, tap the holes for 1/8" metal screws.

Next, insert your 1/8" machine screws into this mold and make sure they are a good snug fit. You will use them later to help separate the boards when the fiddle has been built around the mold.

Now re-assemble the mold. Give it a light sanding, and you have finished with Mold No. 1.

Mold No. 2

This mold will be used later in the construction of the fiddle. Start with a board 1/2" thick x 11" x 15". Trace the outline from your template onto this board. The spots where the head and heel and corner blocks go must be cut 1/2" larger than they were on the first mold. Drill holes in this mold the same way you drilled them in Mold No. 1.

Now, draw two lines, each one measuring 1/2" from the exact center of this mold. Then cut two blocks, 3" x1¼", out of scrap or leftover material. Drill six holes in each block so that the holes will line up over the three sections of the mold that you have drawn out.

DRILLING COUNTER SINK

DRILLING SCREW HOLES

SCREWS IN PLACE

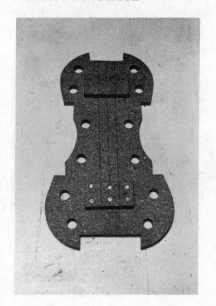

MOLD CUT AND TAKEN APART

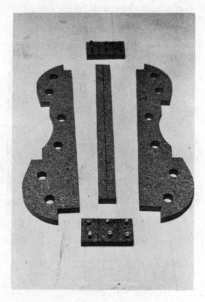

Now screw the metal screws through these blocks and down into the mold itself. When you have done this with both blocks, unscrew the blocks and take them off again. Now cut out the center strip marked by the two lines you have drawn. All that is left to do is to re-assemble the mold. You have a mold that comes apart very easily.

MOLD IS REASSEMBLED.
ANYBODY CAN DO IT

Building the Fiddle

When you are building a fiddle, your first task is to carve the neck and scroll. This is a long, tedious job. It is perhaps one of the most difficult operations you will undertake, and patience is a key requirement. You have to take each step carefully, one by one.

A MACHINE MADE NECK MAKES A GOOD MODEL

SCROLLS BY FAMOUS MAKERS

Estradivario   Guarneri   Amati   Guadagnini   Maggini   Ruggieri

First you will need a block of wood—preferably maple or some other hardwood. This block measures 10¼" long x 2" deep x 1¾" wide. Begin by taking your template and tracing around it on the block of wood. Then you cut along this outline, cutting out the shape of the neck. Use your coping saw and cut very carefully, making sure that the coping saw is at perfect right angles to the wood.

**HEAD CUT AND
DRILLED**

The next major step is to carve the channel where the strings and tuning pegs tie in together. This is a weak point in the head and so it must be done first. It's wise to drill holes clear through the block before you start carving. The tuning pegs will go in these holes later. Drill them with a 3/16" drill bit. When you begin carving the channel for the strings, the holes will be helpful as guides to let you know when you have gone far enough. You must carve the channel until you get to those holes, and then carve so that there is about 1/16" clearance underneath the holes. This gives plenty of clearance for the strings later, when the instrument is tuned.

CHANNAL IS
CARVED

After you have carved the channel and cleaned it out thoroughly, your next step is to carve the scroll. This is not difficult, but is takes lots of time and patience. Most of the cutting is done with a small saw, cutting in circles around the scroll, as shown in the photographs. At all times you must make sure that your cutting is symmetrical on both sides, so that the completed scroll will have a nice, even look.

After you've done the preliminary cutting, do the finishing with a small chip knife. Then use sandpaper to smooth out all cuts and marks and to give the scroll a fine appearance.

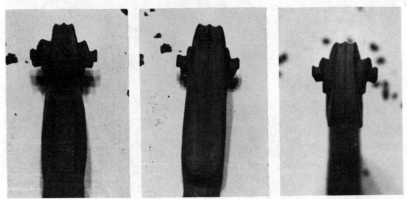

THE SCROLL IS FINISHED BY CHIP CARVING. BE SURE ALL CARVING IS SYMMETRICAL FROM ALL ANGLES

Next, carve the heel so that it will later fit perfectly into the top of the fiddle. Measure from the end of the neck according to the diagram, and saw these positions off.

The neck should be 1-3/8" wide at the top, where the fingerboard will later be glued on. On the opposite side it would be 5/8" wide. Mark this off carefully with a ruler, and saw it so that you get a tapered wedge shape. Later, you will fit this wedge into the top of the fiddle, so it is important to cut it as accurately as you can.

When this is done, measure 3/4'' from the spot at the end of the neck where it will join the body later. Start carving the heel from there, up to where it comes into the neck.

Now completely round off the heel, and melt it into the neck. Be sure to keep it smooth and even. Make it look like a natural flow, from the heel into the neck. Do the same where the head comes into the neck. Always try to keep your carving as smooth as possible. When you have it all just right, sand off the neck very carefully. Sand it until the wood feels like silk, and put it aside until later.

Carving the Belly and Back

The belly and back are each made from a suitable piece of wood measuring 3/4'' thick x 9'' wide x 15'' long. This can either be a solid block of wood, or, more commonly, two pieces joined down the center. Sometimes, if a suitable piece of wood is not quite wide enough for a solid belly or back, you can glue two small strips of wood on the bottom where the lower bouts will be. Stradivari used this method in the construction of some of his violins.

GLUING ON TABS
TO WIDEN THE
BELLY

First join the two halves of the belly and the two halves of the back. This is done with a jointer plane. In each case, the sides are joined so that they fit together perfectly.

I might add at this point that the belly or the back can be made out of solid pieces of wood, instead of having a center joint. This is not too uncommon. If you use a solid piece of wood for the belly, you need a piece that has even grain all across its width. The reason fiddles are usually joined at the center is that this enables you to get the closest grained wood in the middle of the fiddle belly.

Holding Device

It is important to make a holding device. This device will hold the belly and back while they are being dished out, as shown in the photographs and diagrams below.

A SUITABLE HOLDING DEVICE

FIDDLE BACK CLAMPED IN THE HOLDING DEVICE

A CLAMPING LIP
B DISHED OUT AND LINED WITH LEATHER
C 1" x 1" BOARD FOR CLAMPING DEVICE IN VICE

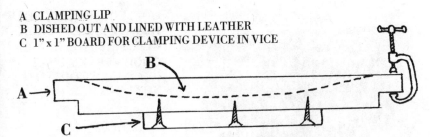

On the fiddle I am making in this book, I am using a solid piece for the belly and two pieces for the back. I am making the belly of one piece because I have a piece of wood which has even grain all the way across it. That is one of the characteristics of red cedar.

If you are gluing the belly sections together, you must be sure to get a perfect joint. Use a jointer plane. The joint should be so perfect that you will not need clamps when you glue the sides together, although it is all right to use clamps if you wish. Almost all the glue should be squeezed out of the joint, and the belly left to dry overnight.

When the belly and back sections have been assembled and glued, put the back aside and work first on the belly. First, using your template, trace the outline of the fiddle on the wood. Then carefully cut it to shape with a coping saw. Or use a band saw, making certain to have the saw at right angles to the wood at all times.

TRACING THE OUTLINE

OUTLINE TRACED, NOTE HOW CORNER IS BROKEN OFF, THIS IS A SIGN OF GOOD VERTICAL GRAINED WOOD WITH NO SLASH.

SAWING TO SHAPE

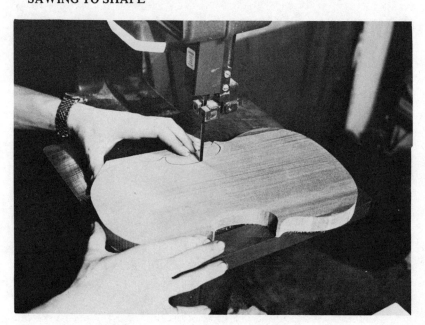

READY FOR CARVING

As shown in the photograph and diagram, the carving goes slowly up the belly. Carve the outside first. Begin at the point where the bridge will be, and carve out slowly, gradually tapering the edge so that it rounds off smoothly. Sometimes the craftsman uses a carving template so he can keep track of how far he's gone and keep to the shape he wants to carve. I do the job completely by visual check until it looks right to me.

REMOVING LOTS OF UNWANTED WOOD THE FAST WAY

SMOOTHING BELLY WITH PLANE

BELLY CARVED SMOOTH, READY FOR SANDING, ALL CURVES ARE MELTED INTO ONE ANOTHER

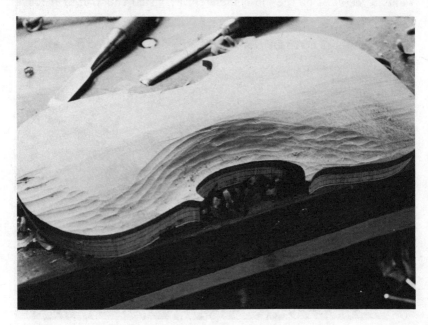

With all your carving, it is very important to keep both sides of fiddle absolutely symmetrical and to maintain a line that flows evenly to the bottom. None of the curves should look unusual or strange. They should have a natural flowing effect, as shown in the photographs of the belly being carved.

After the belly is roughly carved to the desired shape, mark the surface that will be on the inside when finished. Make a mark 1/8" wide completely around the edge. This will later be the edge of the fiddle. Carve a channel for the purfling around the edge, as shown in the photograph.

SOUND HOLES HAVE BEEN DRILLED AND CUT, PURFLING CHANNAL IS CUT

Smooth the belly with scrapers and then sandpaper until it has almost the final finished effect.

Using your template sheet, carefully trace out where the "F" holes will go. Trace them lightly with a pencil so as not to mark the wood too much, and drill the round part of the "F" holes all the way through. Use a very sharp knife to cut out the "F." Be very careful not to let the knife go astray. DO NOT try to cut completely through the face with one cut. Delicately trace the outline with your knife, and keep going around and around, over and over it with the knife, going a little deeper each time until finally you cut through. If you do a clean job with this cutting, you won't have to clean it up too much with sandpaper. Take a small piece of sandpaper folded three times, and clean away any knife cuts you see. But don't sand away too much material and be careful to keep the sound holes symmetrical, each the exact mirror image of the other.

The fiddle face is extremely fragile once the carving is completed, so handle it gently when you are doing the following operations.

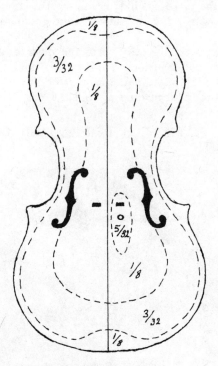

GRADUATION OF THE BELLY

Now, turn the belly over so that you can work on the surface which will be inside the completed fiddle. This surface must be carved until the belly meets the required thicknesses in all places. The fiddle, unlike other instruments, changes its thickness from one point to another. That's why you can't simply plane it.

The belly diagram shows exactly how thick the wood should be at different spots on the belly. You must be very careful to melt these thicknesses into one another, and not have sharp changes in the thickness of the belly. You have to carve very slowly and carefully to avoid going through, for the tolerances are very thin.

The most important tool for doing this delicate job is the fiddle maker's calipers. These are quite expensive to buy. You can use regular outside calipers, but if you do, you will have to use a ruler to check places that are thinner than the edge, to determine how far you have carved. This is extremely difficult. It's quite a problem to keep doing it constantly.

In the section on tools, you will find instructions for making calipers which give you precise thicknesses as needed. Calipers are not hard to make and are definitely worth the time involved in making them.

Fiddle Belly

The last thing you do to the belly—and one of the most important—is to make the base bar. The board used to make the bar should be 3/8" wide by 1" deep by 10" long. This is the only brace that goes inside a fiddle. This is done as shown in the photograph. Place the bar across the belly of the fiddle, using your finger as a guide. With a pencil, trace the inside curvature of the fiddle belly against the piece of wood you are using for a base bar. The final shape is approximately 3/8" wide by 10" long by 3/8" high at the highest point. This piece of wood must be very straight grained.

TRACING THE CURVE OF THE FACE ONTO THE BASS BAR

After you have traced the outline of the curvature onto your piece of wood, you must cut precisely along the mark you have made with your pencil. Then fit it to the fiddle. Keep sanding and scraping the bottom of the piece until it fits the inside of the fiddle perfectly.

When you have achieved a perfect fit, glue the base bar in place, holding it in position with light pressure from two or three clamps. It is a good idea to put a piece of wood between the clamps and the wood of the fiddle, so that the clamps do not mar the fiddle.

GLUING IN THE BASS BAR

After the base bar has dried, carve it to shape as shown in the photo and round it smoothly with sandpaper. The belly is now finished and you can put it aside until later.

BASS BAR IS CARVED TO ITS FINAL SHAPE

Carving the Back

You carve the back much as you carved the belly. First trace the outline of the back onto the wood. Remember to leave a tab of wood at the end. This tab later becomes part of the heel of the fiddle.

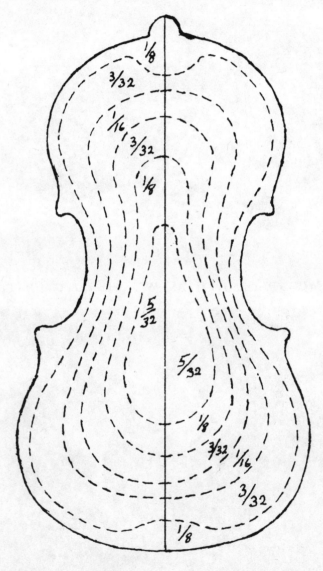

GRADUATION OF THE BACK

THE BACK IS CARVED JUST LIKE THE BELLY

WASTE WOOD IS REMOVED FAST WITH ROUND BOTTOM PLANE

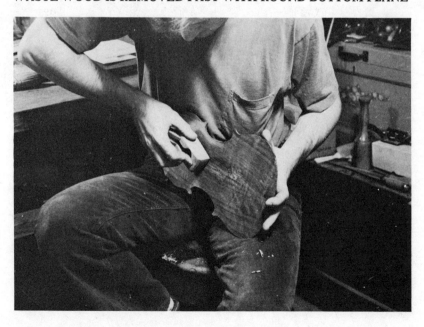

The main difference between carving the back and carving the belly is that the back is made of much harder wood. Therefore, carving it takes longer.

First carve the outside to shape. Try to match it to the shape you carved for the belly as closely as possible. After this is done, turn it around and carve out the inside. Once again, use your calipers and cut very slowly and carefully.

You will notice, as shown in the diagram, that the thicknesses are different from the thicknessess of the belly. Adhere to these very precisely.

After the back has been completely carved, sand it and lay it aside until later.

Building the Corpse

Now you are ready to make the sides of the fiddle. Cut the sides to the dimensions shown. Now, using scrapers and a plane, thin them until they are exactly 1/16'' thick everywhere.

The sides of the fiddle are made of six pieces: two for the upper bouts, two longer pieces for the lower bouts, and the shortest pieces, referred to as the "C's"—in all, three pieces to each completed side. After these have been cut and thinned, they can be put aside until it is time to bend them.

Corner Blocks

The corner blocks are made out of straight-grained wood. They are split with a large chisel, as shown in the photograph. The grain must run straight up and down. This insures that you can carve the corner blocks to shape, to match the outline of the fiddle.

SPLITTING CORNER BLOCKS

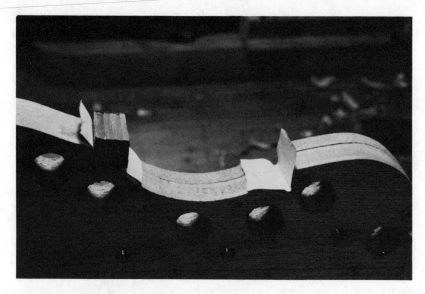

SPLIT CORNER BLOCKS

Heel Block and Tail Block

These are made out of two blocks of hard wood with the grain going from right to left. Carve them to the dimensions shown on the template.

GLUING IN CORNER BLOCKS WITH PAPER

CORNER BLOCKS MARKED FOR CARVING

Now, you have to fit all corners of the fiddle into the mold. Fit the corners of the "C's" and also the head and heel blocks into the mold and glue them in place, with papers in between the mold and the heel and head, and other papers between the mold and the corner blocks. These blocks are only glued to the lower section of the mold—that is, the half of the mold which is thicker. The other half must not have any glue on it, because it has to be removed later. Don't use too much glue—just enough to hold the blocks in place during construction.

When you have the blocks glued exactly in the right places, trace the shape of the fiddle on them, using your template sheet. Cut on the traced line with a sharp knife, so that the corners follow the precise contours of the fiddle.

Now it is time to bend the sides. But you can't use a bending iron, as previously described in this book, for bending fiddle sides. The curves are too sharp to be bent on a bending iron. Instead, use a soldering iron.

BENDING THE SIDES

First, boil the sides in a pot with a cover on it, with a weight on the wood to keep it level in the water. They should be boiled for about half an hour. After they've been boiled, they will bend easily around a soldering iron, and hold their shape quite well.

The best soldering iron for your purpose is the very large one, 1/2" to 3/4" in diameter. A smaller one will work, but it is easier with a large one. Clamp your soldering iron to a table or put it in a vice, to hold it while you use it for bending.

As you bend these sides and "C's," keep them exactly to the shape of the fiddle template. First bend the "C's" to shape, as shown in the photograph. Then bend the upper bout and the lower bout. When all sections are bent, leave them to dry for two to three days so that no dampness is left in them.

Now you are ready to assemble the body. First, clamp the "C's" in place, using rope for clamping. Do a dry run without glue, to make certain everything fits. Then remove the "C's" and apply glue to the corner block. Be sure the glue doesn't run off onto the mold itself, as this would make it extremely difficult to remove the sides from the mold when you are finished. Position the "C's and tie them in place. Allow the glue four to five hours to set.

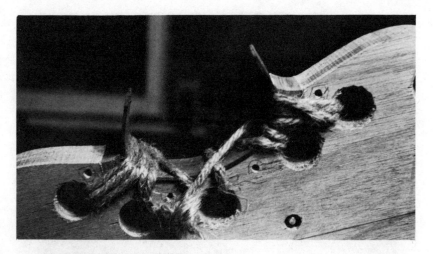

GLUING "C" IN PLACE

When the glue is completely dry, take a sharp knife and trim the "C's" off flush with the corner blocks, as shown in the picture.

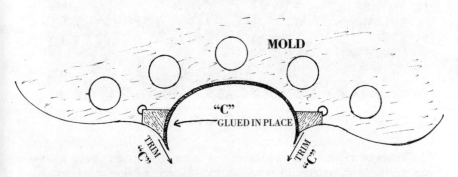

MOLD

"C"
GLUED IN PLACE

TRIM "C"

TRIM "C"

The next step is to glue the lower bouts in place. Match them up perfectly with the corner blocks so that the joint is even and closed. There must be no gaps. Start again with a dry run to make sure you get a good fit. When the fit is satisfactory, remove the sides. Apply glue to the heel block and to the side of one of the corner blocks, and glue that lower bout on. Do the same with the other lower bout. Be sure to keep the joint between the two lower bouts closed, as this line will show later in the finished fiddle. Allow at least four or five hours for the glue to set completely, and then remove the clamps.

GLUING UPPER AND LOWER BOUTS

The next step is to glue on the upper bouts. These don't need to have as perfect a fit as the other blocks, for the top section will be sawed away later when the neck is glued in place. Allow them four or five hours to dry.

Now remove the bottom section of the mold. To do this, first unscrew the eight bolts that hold the two sections of the mold together. Then turn the mold over, and insert three screws into the threads that you tapped in the first part of the mold. When you screw these all the way down, you will force the second part of the mold out. If you haven't spilled any glue in the previous operation, this will be relatively simple and the bottom should come out easily.

REMOVING BOLTS WHICH HOLD THE MOLD TOGETHER

USING BOLTS TO SEPARATE THE MOLD

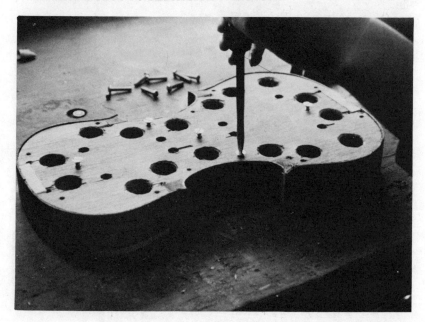

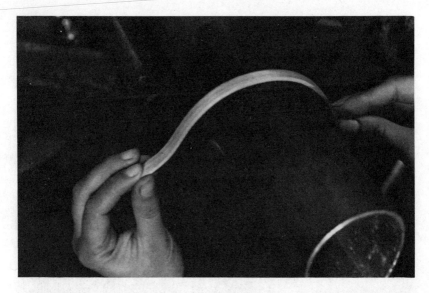

BENDING THE LINING

At this point, you have the lower section of the mold (the thicker section) with the sides attached to it. Part of the sides will be protruding from the edge of the mold. This is where your first linings will be glued on.

SECTION OF MOLD REMOVED

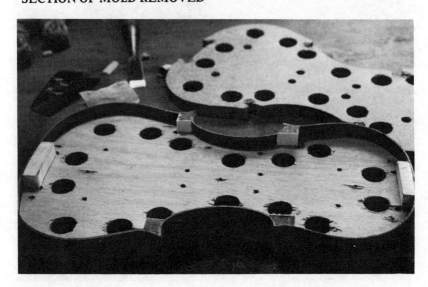

Now all linings must be cut to size—that is, 1/2" wide by 3/4" deep, and the length is equal to the length of the sides to which they will be attached. After you have cut them, bend them the same way you bent the sides. Now fit them into the sides and into the corner blocks and the head and heel blocks, as shown in the diagram. Fit them closely and do a good job, for this is what secures the belly and bottom of the fiddle to the sides.

LININGS READY TO BE FITTED

Glue the linings in place, using pegs (clothes pins) for clamps. Leave everything to dry for four to six hours.

PAPER SCRAPED AWAY TO ALLOW GLUING OF THE LININGS

GLUING IN LININGS

When the glue is completely dry, remove the pins and clamps. The linings are planed and sanded square with the edges of the side.

After the linings have been put into the top half of the fiddle, the rest of the mold must be removed. To do this, take a hot knife (heated over a hot flame or on an electric stove), and insert it into the glue joints of the corner blocks of the mold. Do this carefully, slowly applying a gentle, steady pressure until you can feel the corner blocks and the head and heel blocks break away from the mold. Once all these blocks are loosened, they can be taken from the mold.

BREAKING OFF THE MOLD

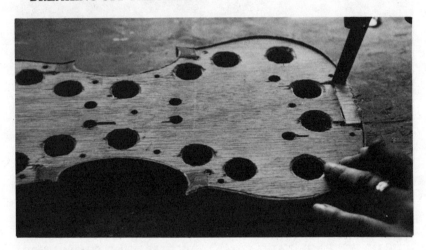

FIRST MOLD REMOVED

Now the second mold is put in, replacing the first one. Put it down, up against the first lining you have glued in. Then get the fiddle sides properly secured in the second mold.

SECOND MOLD IN PLACE

Next, bend and fit the linings for the other side of the fiddle. This is done exactly the way you did the first set of linings.

Now there is one thing left to do before the final assembly of the body. You must cut a mortice in the head block to receive the neck. Some people do this after the body is assembled, using knives, saws, and chisels, but it is simpler if it is done now.

Using the diagram shown here, mark the top of the fiddle to the dimensions shown. Then, with your backsaw, cut into the top 1/4'' on each mark. After that, take a chisel and clean out the mortice so that it is flush all the way down to 1/4''. Now you are ready to glue on the back.

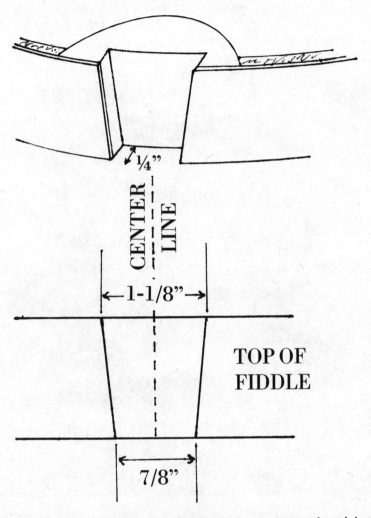

CENTER LINE

¼"

←1-1/8"→

TOP OF FIDDLE

7/8"

After you have cut the mortice for the neck, you are ready to join the back of the fiddle to the sides. First make sure that the back and sides match up perfectly and that there is no gap. The sides must be true to the back all the way around. Use a small plane and sanding sticks to get your fit right.

When the fit is perfect, drill two small holes through the back. Drill one near where the neck will be, and one down at the base of the fiddle. You will insert small dowel sticks or round tooth picks through these holes. You use these to line up the back perfectly, where it goes onto the sides.

When the back is lined up precisely, and you have a good fit all around, remove the back again, apply glue, and clamp it in place. For this job you need to tie the back down with rope.

Let the back dry overnight. When the glue is completely dry, take the mold out of the fiddle sides and you will now have the sides and back glued together. Clean up excess glue with a small scraper or knife, and sandpaper the entire inside of the fiddle clean and smooth again. This is the time to add a label, if you wish to put your name on your fiddle. Place the label on the left hand side of the fiddle back, so that the sound hole in the belly will be placed directly above it. That way, the label will show through the sound hole. Anybody can easily read it and see who made this fiddle.

Gluing on the Belly

You do this the same way you glued the back onto the sides, except that now you are working without a mold, and so the fit **must** be perfect. If it isn't perfect, you will bend the body of the fiddle out of shape. Check and re-check your fit, using sanding sticks and a small plane until the belly is matched perfectly to the sides.

Now position it as it will finally go, and drill two holes: one where the neck joins, and the other below at the base of the fiddle. Apply glue. Using small dowels or toothpicks through the holes as guides, glue the belly in place and leave it to dry overnight.

GLUING THE CORPS TOGETHER

When it is dry, you are finished with your fiddle body—or corpse, as it is called—and you are ready to go on to the next step of fitting the neck.

Fitting the Neck

The first thing to do in fitting the neck is to decide the angle at which it will lie in relation to the body. This is shown in the diagram.

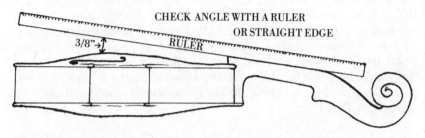

CHECK ANGLE WITH A RULER
OR STRAIGHT EDGE

RULER

3/8"

At this stage you must not forget to compensate for the extra thickness of the finger board so that you don't wind up with the neck too high.

Next, the heel is cut to the proper angle, as shown on the template for the neck in the rear of the book.

The end of the heel must next be cut to the same taper as the mortice in the top of the fiddle. Once this is done, you can roughly carve the heel round, but leave plenty of wood for final fitting after the neck is on the body.

The neck should now fit into the mortice snugly. Squeeze it into place and check the angle of the neck with a ruler. The ruler should clear the belly by 3/8 of an inch where the bridge will go (between the nicks in the "F" holes), as shown in the diagram.

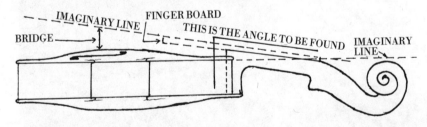

IMAGINARY LINE   FINGER BOARD
THIS IS THE ANGLE TO BE FOUND   IMAGINARY LINE
BRIDGE

Adjust the neck until this angle is achieved. After the fit is perfect, apply glue to the mortice and glue on the neck, using one clamp as shown in the photograph. After the glue has dried, remove the clamp and carve the heelbutton up to the bottom of the neck. Carve it round and smooth.

GLUING NECK ON BODY

Making the Fingerboard

Next, take the blank of wood for the fingerboard, and plane the bottom smooth and flat. Then shape the fingerboard to its final shape as shown in the template sheet. After the fingerboard is shaped, glue it onto the neck with three or four clamps, as shown in the photograph. Use small pieces of scrap wood between the clamps and fingerboard so as not to mark the fingerboard with the clamps. After the glue is dry, trim the edges of the neck smooth with the fingerboard and carve the neck to its final shape.

GLUING FINGER BOARD ON THE NECK

Now the fiddle needs a final fitting up. The saddle is fitted into the base of the belly. The saddle can be made out of hardwood or bone. A hole is then drilled in the bottom of the fiddle for the end pin, which will hold the tailpiece.

BONE SADDLE INLAYED INTO BELLY

Fitting the tuning pegs must be done with a special reamer and peg shaper. These are very expensive to buy, so if you are not planning on making more instruments, they are not worth purchasing. You can have this job done for you by an instrument maker or repair man.

REAMING THE PEG HOLES   SNAPPING THE TUNING PEGS

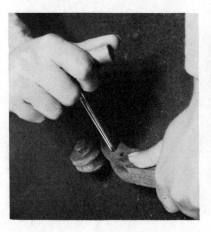
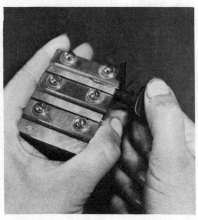

Next the nut is made by placing a small blank of hardwood or bone against the end of the fingerboard on the peg head, and with a pencil tracing the shape of the fingerboard onto the blank. The blank is then cut to that shape so that it will rise above the fingerboard about 1/16". Then the fours grooves are cut for the strings to ride in.

Fitting the Sound Post

This is a small dowel made out of a piece of straight-grained spruce or cedar, 5/16" in diameter.

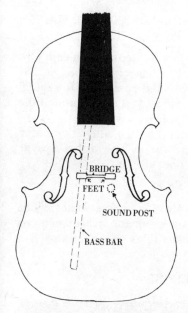

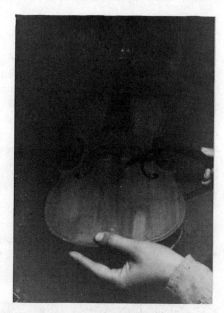

The length of the sound post will depend on the depth of the fiddle at the place where it will go. This length is found be using calipers on the fiddle at the place where the sound post will go. See diagrams. Using the calipers, mark the sound post to that length, then subtract from that length the thickness of the belly and back (about 5/16").

Placing the Sound Post

The sound post is set right in line with the foot of the bridge, about 1/4" behind the bridge. Putting it in is tricky. You can use a sound post setter shown in the chapter on tools, or you can make a similar tool out of a coat hanger.

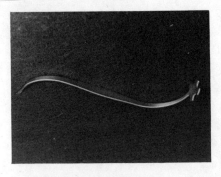 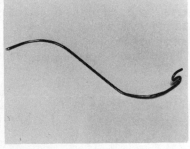

SOUND POST SETTER   SOUND POST SETTER MADE
                            FROM A COAT HANGER

The first step is to impale the sound post on the setter, then carefully put it through the sound hole and wedge it in place. Then wiggle the setter gently until it comes loose from the sound post. Take the setter and turn it around, and, using this other end and working through the sound hole, push the post gently into place.

The position of the sound post will affect the tone quality. The closer it is to the bridge foot, the brighter the tone will be. The farther away it is from the bridge foot, the richer the tone will be.

Fitting the Bridge

The feet of the bridge must be trimmed with a knife so that they fit flush with the face. After this is done, string up the instrument and adjust the height of the strings. The treble strings should be closer to the fingerboard than the bass strings.

SETTING THE HEIGHT OF THE BRIDGE

After all this is accomplished, you must unstring the fiddle, remove and store the tuning pegs, bridge, tail pin and tail piece. Then the whole instrument is sanded and finished. Refer to the chapter on finishing.

INLAYING AND DESIGN

When an instrument is well made, it truly is a thing of beauty even if it is very plain; but an instrument with tasteful and well executed ornamentation is a work of art. I am showing in the following photographs some instruments which I hope will spark your imagination and set you in the right direction.

These first two photographs are of a Hardanger fiddle.

This instrument has extensive pen and ink drawing over the belly, sides, back and head. The drawing is perfectly symmetrical on all parts of the instrument. If you wish to do this type of work, the instrument must first have a sealing coat of finish to prevent the ink from blotching in the wood grain. Needless to say, you must be a fine artist with rock steady hands. In the next photograph is a close-up view of the tail piece (and a crack in need of repair) of this fiddle. Note how well the inlays are set into the ebony with no filler. Only the best of craftsmen can achieve this closeness of fit. The inlays are ivory, abalone shell and mother-of-pearl.

This next photograph is of a lute mandolin (Tater Bug). This mandolin was made by the Vega Company around 1900-1910, when fine inlay was a must. The edge of the fretboard is bound in ivory with maple binding and black, white, black, white, black, white and black purfling around the edge of the face. The inlays in the ebony fretboard are engraved mother-of-pearl, and the oval sound hole is rimmed with white celluloid, with a rosette made of black, white, black purfling and abalone shell. The pick guard is tortoise shell, laid with mother-of-pearl vines, flowers and leaves. This is all inlaid into the face of the instrument. This is a fine example of what used to be common workmanship.

This next photograph is of a fingerboard that I made for one of my guitars. It is an ebony fingerboard with mother-of-pearl inlays which I copied from an old banjo inlay pattern. It is quite common to copy old instruments; if you wish too, feel free to copy any of the designs shown in this book. Or, you may have your own ideas.

The following photograph is of an old Kay mandolin. The head is overlaid with imitation (linoleum) mother-of-pearl, and was then engraved with a pattern around the edge and the words "Kay Kraft". This engraving was then painted in with gold. On the face of the body is a reef painted in gold and brown over the finish. I imagine this was done with the help of a stencil, as I have seen other instruments with the same design.

These last two photographs are of an inlaid dulcimer that I made. I don't know for certain if anyone has ever used this idea of negative inlays, but I imagine that it must have been done before. I did this by cutting the mother-of-pearl into squares that fit inside the fret positions. Then I cut out the picture in the center and inlaid it into the ebony fretboard with epoxy filler paste as I will describe later in this chapter.

Materials for Ornamentation

There are many things that can be used for ornamentation and inlay, such as mother-of-pearl, abalone shell, bone, ivory, veneer woods, copper, silver, gold, stone, paint, ink, and more. I will describe here the most common materials starting with mother-of-pearl and abalone shell. As you can see in the photograph, it is sold be luthier suppliers as thin sheets which are about .050 inch thick. You can grind your own abalone shell to the thickness that you want, but it is very harmful to your lungs to breathe in the dust. Also, the time spent grinding it could be put to better use, since the sheets are quite reasonably priced. Abalone can also be bought in squares or dots ready for inlaying. It can be pre-cut into thin strips ready for inlaying lines. Mother-of-pearl is also sold as pre-cut inlays as shown on the next two pages. If you want to you could copy these designs in abalone shell, ivory, gold or silver.

MOTHER OF PEARL AND ABALONE SHELL IS SOLD LIKE THIS

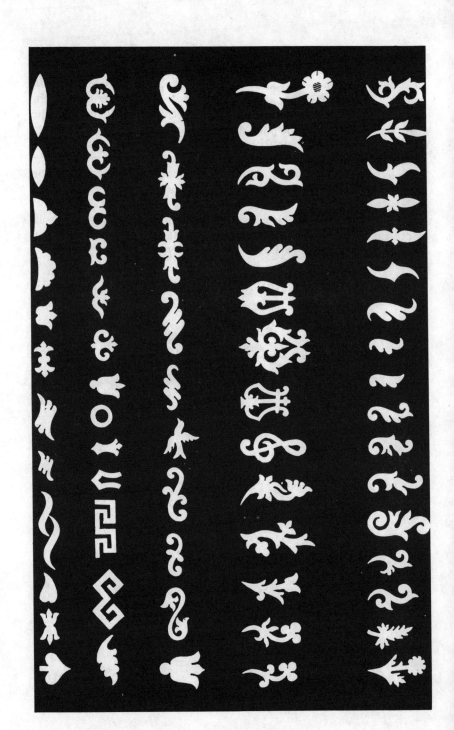

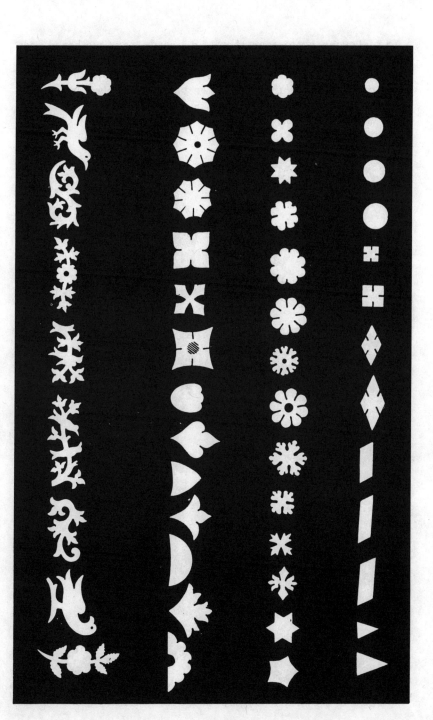

177

The following photograph shows nine ready-made mother-of-pearl rosettes. These are set into black wood and come ready for inlaying. Also in this type of pre-made inlays are the following head veneers. These do not come as they are shown but are pre-inlaid into square sheets of black veneer. All you need do is glue them to your head and cut it to the shape you desire.

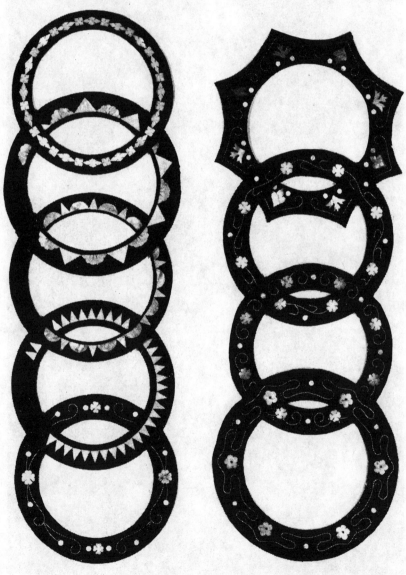

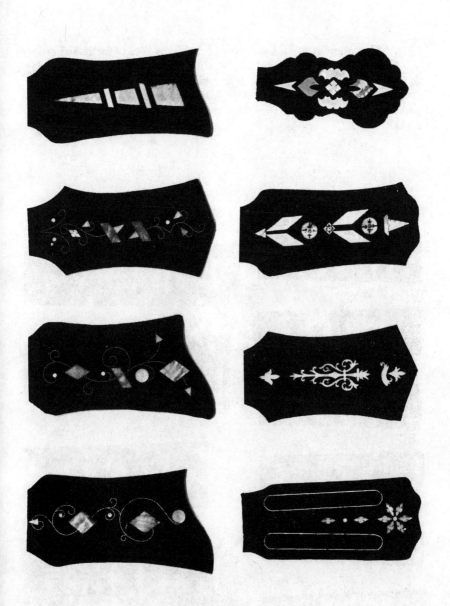

This next photograph shows some of the many sets of fretboard inlays available. These come to you ready cut; all you need to do is to inlay them into your fretboard. Now if you wanted these patterns in abalone shell or some other material, you would have to make them yourself. I personally would rather originate my own design and do the work myself.

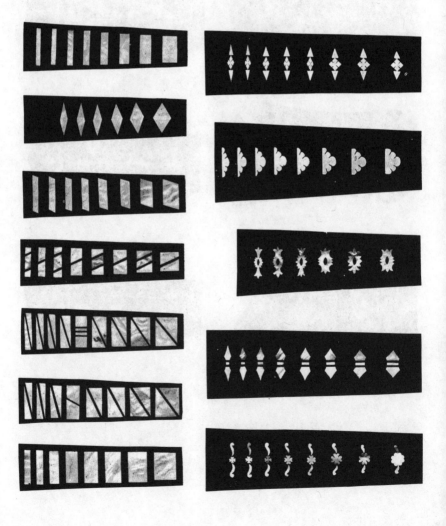

Bone and Ivory

Ivory can be bought from piano suppliers in the form of coverings for piano keys. These can then be cut into inlays.

Bone is available in narrower strips as sold for guitar bridge saddles, and these can also be used for inlays. Bone is also sold as small round dowels which are very useful for making position dots on the face or the side of fretboards.

Wood and Veneer

Wood veneers are sold in sheets and rolls by cabinet suppliers and in good lumber yards. Many exotic woods can be bought this way. They come in different thicknesses such as 1/28", 1/16", 1/8" and 1/4". They can be used for many purposes, such as making purfling, rosette tiles, head veneers, pick guards and marquetry inlays. Purfling is available from luthier supply houses and it comes as shown in this photograph. From left to right, these are black - white - black, brown - black and white slanted squares; black and white squares; black and white slanted squares; and the ever popular black and white herringbone. Also available from suppliers are ready made rosettes. These come in many colors and designs ready for inlaying; all you need do is cut a channel in the face around where your sound hole will go and glue your rosette into place. The quality of these varies with the price. These rosettes are made from wood veneer, usually holly wood that has been dyed various colors.

SHEETS OF VENEER WOOD

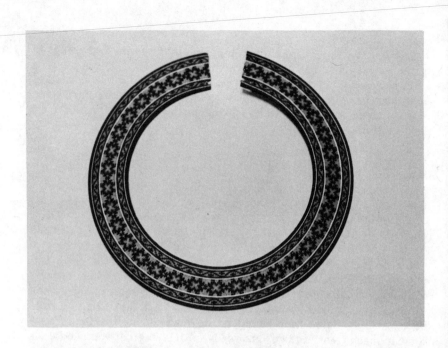

THESE ARE READY MADE WOOD ROSETTES

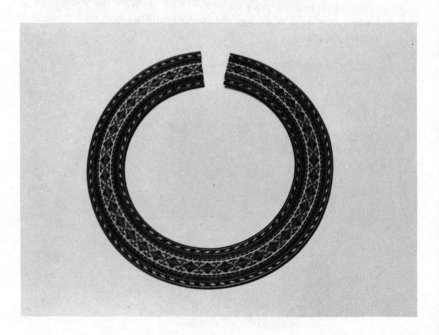

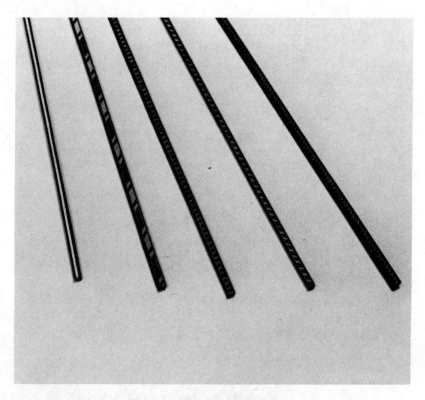

STRIPS OF PURFLING AS THEY ARE SOLD

Making Mosaic Tiles for the Rosette

The first step in making a rosette is designing the tile. After you have made your drawing as shown in this simplified drawing, you must take 8'' lengths of 1/16'' thick veneer in the colors you wish and cut them into strips 1/16'' wide. Next, you must lay these strips in the order they will go in. These are then glued together into a plank. Do all this gluing on a piece of waxed paper to avoid unwanted sticking. Glue all your planks together and keep them in order. Be stingy with the glue. After all the planks are dry, they are glued one on top of the other. At this time your pattern should be apparent at the end of the block. If you wish, you can glue this up between two carved and waxed pieces of wood so that your block will have a natural curve to it. This will make it easier to fit the tiles into the rosette. The last thing left now is to saw this block into slices 1/16'' thick. The tiles are now ready for inlaying.

DESIGN IS DRAWN

1/16'' STRIPS ARE LAID IN ORDER

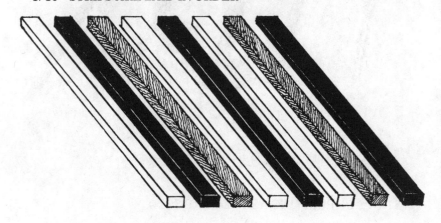

THE FIRST "PLANK" IS GLUED UP

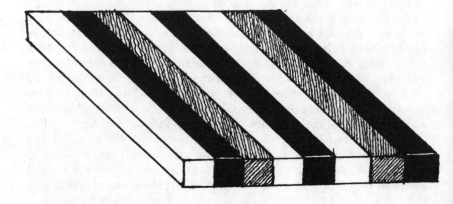

"PLANKS" ARE STACKED AND GLUED

TILES ARE THEN SAWED OFF

This following photograph shows various tiles which were made in this manner.

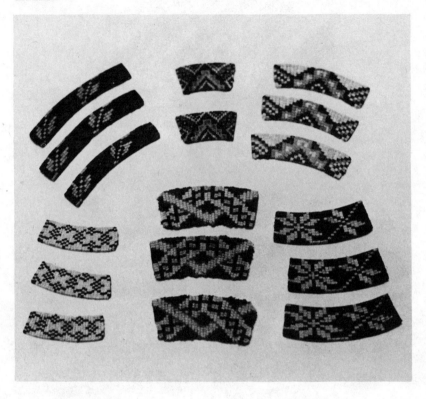

Making the Rosette

There are different ways of making a rosette. I will show you my way. The first step is to measure the width of your tiles and the purflings you will use in making your rosette. Next, with a knife or circle cutter, cut the channel for the rosette. These cuts should be 1/16" deep. After cuttings, the channel must be routed to a depth of 1/16". This can be done with a power router or a chisel. Now when the channel is cut you must bend your purfling on the bending iron to the diameter of the channel. You must be careful, in bending the purfling, not to break it or to let it overheat and come apart. It should be wet for bending, but not soaked.

CUTTING THE CIRCLE

ROUTING THE CHANNEL

BENDING THE PURFLING

Next, the purflings are glued into place, using push pins to hold them until the glue is dry. After the glue has dried, remove the push pins and plane the surface of the purfling level with the face. Then the tiles must be glued in place one at a time. It will be necessary to trim them with a sharp knife so they will fit together well. After all the titles are in and the glue is dry, sand and scrape the rosette level with the face.

GLUING THE PURFLING

GLUING IN THE TILES

SAND LEVEL

CUT SOUND HOLE

The following picture is of a rosette made in the same way, using abalone tiles that were cut with a jeweler's saw.

The next photograph is of a rosette made a little differently. With this one, as you can see, a drawing was made first, and then the inlays on the drawing were traced onto tracing paper. The tracing was then glued onto a suitable piece of abalone shell of mother-of-pearl. This was then cut out carefully with a jeweler's saw. The inlays were then glued in their place in the routed channels; at this point the purfling was already in. The black background was made by grating a small piece of charcoal into a fine powder; the powder was then sifted to be sure that there were no lumps. Next, epoxy glue was mixed, then the powder was mixed into the epoxy. This makes a heavy, thick paste like tar which was then spread in place around and over the inlays. This was then left overnight to harden. Finally, it was sanded down until it was level with the face, first using coarse sandpaper and a sanding block, and then using fine sandpaper until the whole surface was smooth.

Wood Marquetry

This is the art of making pictures or designs in wood by using veneers. These next photographs show a rosette and two head veneers ready to be used. The rosette will need to be cut round before use.

These are quite simple to make. The first thing to do is to draw your design on a sheet of paper. You will need one piece of dark veneer wood, one piece of light veneer wood, and a piece of 1/16'' plywood. This plywood is available in hobby stores; it is usually used for making models. These pieces must then be stacked one on top of the other as shown, with the drawing glued to the first veneer. These are then taped together securely with masking tape. Next, drill a very small hole through the whole stack at a place where it will be the least noticeable. Then, with your jeweler's saw (blade threaded through the hole) saw out your pattern. Be careful to keep your saw vertical while sawing. When you are done sawing, remove the tape and dismantle the stack. Then put the light veneer picture in the dark veneer background, and vice versa with the other, discarding the plywood. This process resembles a jigsaw puzzle, and you get two pictures for the price of one.

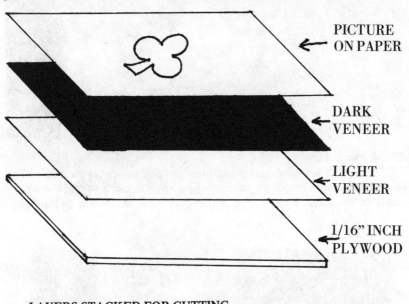

← PICTURE
ON PAPER

← DARK
VENEER

← LIGHT
VENEER

← 1/16'' INCH
PLYWOOD

LAYERS STACKED FOR CUTTING

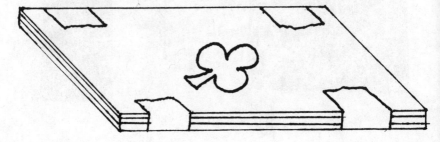

 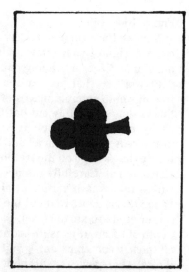

THE RESULT IS TWO WOOD PICTURES

Fretboard Inlays [Position markers]

Inlaying dots is the most common way to mark positions. On a guitar, the positions that can be marked with dots are the 3rd, 5th, 7th, 9th, 12th, 15th, and 19th. On a mandolin, they are the 3rd, 5th, 7th, 10th, and 12th. Inlaying dots is easy. You simply drill shallow holes in the fretboards the same size as your dots, the glue the dots in position. Allow the glue to dry and sand the fretboard level and smooth as shown in the photograph. You are now ready to hammer in your frets.

INLAYING BONE DOTS

Fancy Inlay Work

Now we have come to my favorite part. The first thing to do is to draw out a design of your inlays. After this is done, trace these sections of inlay onto pieces of tracing paper. Remember to number all sections of your work so that you can easily put it back together. Glue all you tracings onto suitable pieces of abalone shell or mother-of-pearl. After this is done, carefully cut out the designs with your jeweler's saw. Go easily now, as the shell is very fragile and will break if too much pressure is used. When all of the inlays have been cut, lay them exactly where they will go on the fretboard and trace around their outline with a sharp pencil. Carefully remove all the inlays and put them aside. Now, with a thin, sharp knife, cut all these outlines as perfectly as you can. When this is done, rout out the spaces for the inlays with a small hobby router or sharp small chisel. Save all the wood chips that you can. The depth of this routing is the same as the thickness of your shell. Now take all those wood chips and grind them up with a mortar and pestle until they are fine powder. Sift them like flour so that no large pieces remain, then mix this powder with epoxy glue until you have a thick paste. Fill all the inlay positions with paste and push the inlays into place. This will force out the paste, thereby filling any gaps or faults in your routing. Leave this overnight to harden. Then, using a sanding block, level the entire fretboard and inlays. Finally using No. 320, No. 400 and No. 600 wet and dry sandpaper with three-in-one oil, sand the entire fretboard until it is polished all over. Clean out all the fret slots and hammer in the frets.

INLAY PATTERN IS TRACED
AND THEN GLUED TO SHELL

INLAYS ARE CUT OUT

INLAYS ARE ASSEMBLED IN THE APPROPRIATE PLACES AND
TRACED AROUND FOR INLAYING

AFTER ROUTING THE
INLAYS ARE GLUED
IN PLACE, THEN
SANDED LEVEL

195

On the following pages you will find more standard old inlay patterns.

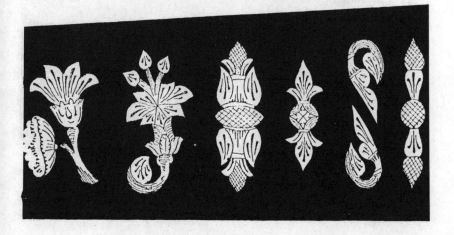

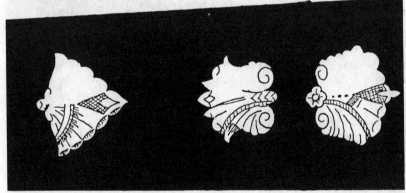

Binding and Edge Purfling

The photograph above shows a guitar with a single strip of rosewood binding. Binding usually measures 1/4'' deep by 1/8'' wide. Any number of hardwoods can be used for a binding; for example, rosewood, maple, or walnut. To put a binding on, a groove must be cut around the edge of the instrument. This can be done by hand with a purfling cutter and chisel, or with a power router with a guide set up. The diagram below shows what the groove must look like for a single binding. After the groove is cut, the binding is bent to shape and glued in place using masking tape to hold it until the glue is dry. Then the tape is removed and the binding is scraped and sanded level with the surface of the instrument.

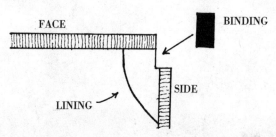

If you wish to do a double binding (a binding with a strip of purfling) you will need to cut two grooves—one for the purfling and one for the binding, as shown in the diagram. The purfling is glued on first and held in place with push pins. Then the binding is glued down with masking tape to hold it in place. When the glue is dry, the tape is removed and the purfling and binding are scraped and sanded level with the surfaces of the instrument.

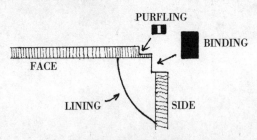

GLUING PURFLING IN PLACE WITH PUSH PINS TO HOLD IT UNTIL THE GLUE IS DRY

FINISHING

Sanding

The first step toward good finishing is to have the instrument smooth and even all over. This is done by sanding with various grades of sandpaper. Sandpaper is used in three ways. One is with the sandpaper folded three times and rubbed around the instrument with your palm or fingertips. This would be for sanding the sides, neck, heel and other not-flat surfaces. A second way is with the sandpaper tacked to a small flat sanding block. This would be used for sanding the face, back, head and other flat surfaces. A third way to use sandpaper is to use it glued to either flat or curved sticks. The sandpaper can be glued to these sanding sticks with disk adhesive, which can be bought in most hardware and auto parts stores. The sanding sticks are used for sanding places such as fiddle sides, scrolls, inside the pegbox, the joint between the neck and sides, and all hard to reach surfaces.

Start by sanding your instrument all over with No. 80 sandpaper. Always try to sand with the grain—that is, in the direction that the grain runs. After you have sanded the whole instrument with No. 80 sandpaper, change over to No. 120 sandpaper and sand the entire instrument with that. Next, sand the entire instrument with No. 220 sandpaper. The instrument will now be smooth all over. Take a damp (not wet) rag and wipe the entire instrument; this will show up any flaws in your sanding. Go over these flaws again until they are gone.

Filling

Porous woods such as rosewood, mahogany and walnut will need to be filled. Non-porous woods such as maple, cedar and spruce must not be filled. Paste filler is available in cans from hardware stores. It can be bought in a variety of shades from clear to black. Choose one that is a shade darker than the wood you are filling, and follow the directions on the can. After the filler has dried, you must re-sand all the parts of the instrument that have been filled. After this is done, the instrument is ready for the finish.

Finishing: Oil, Varnish, Lacquer or French Polish?

The simplest finish is an oil finish. All you will need is a rag, a can of Watco Danish oil, and little or no talent. The results will be a natural non-gloss finish that is quite pleasant to look at.

Varnish produces a nice, deep protective finish that looks good. However, it is a real pain to use since it takes forever to dry well, it picks up dust while it is drying, and it is hard to rub to a high gloss; but if it is not laid on too thickly, it will really produce a fine sounding instrument. For varnishing, you will need a good quality soft hair brush, oil varnish and turpentine.

Lacquer is the most popular finish used by guitar makers and factories. The advantage of using lacquer is that time is saved in the finishing process. Lacquer, when finished properly, is very beautiful. When working lacquer (sanding coats) there is no long wait for drying. The thing I don't like about it, however, is the way it kills the tone of the instrument. A good idea is to finish the neck, back and sides of the instrument with lacquer, and French polish the face (sounding board) with a thin coat of rubber lacquer. Another drawback to using lacquer is that it must be sprayed on with a compressor and spray gun or air brush. Don't use canned spray lacquer. I don't know why, but all of it is junk. A good reason for using lacquer is that it is very protective of the instrument.

French polishing is my favorite method of finishing an instrument. All you will need for the process are shellac flakes and alcohol or rubbing lacquer, and some pieces of lint free cloth (old diapers), a plastic squeeze bottle and some rubber bands. It finishes to a high gloss that is not too thick, and so it does not hurt the tone and volume of the instrument. But it does take a little practice to do it right.

Finishing With Oil

Oil finish is the easiest to do. The best product that I have found for this is Wadco Danish Oil Finish. This product is available in any well-stocked hardware store.

After the instrument has been completely sanded, simply wipe the oil all over (except on the fingerboard) with a lint free rag, and hang it up to dry for about four hours. After is has dried thoroughly, sand it lightly all over with No. 400 wet and dry sandpaper. Then re-coat it with oil as you did the first coat. Let this coat dry overnight and you are done. You can now sring your new toy.

Finishing With Varnish

For a varnish finish, you will need turpentine for thinning and for cleaning your brush. Also, you will need a good quality soft brush which can be bought in an art supply shop. I use one that I made with human hair tied to the stick with thread. It is the best brush I have ever used. You will also need some No. 600 wet and dry sandpaper and powdered rotten stone. This is available in most paint stores.

HANGING AN INSTRUMENT TO DRY

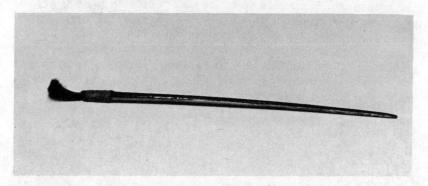

HOME MADE VARNISH BRUSH, HUMAN HAIR

There are basically two kinds of varnish: spirit varnish (short oil varnish) and oil varnish (long oil varnish). Oil varnish is best for the tone of the instrument, but requires working in warm, dry weather, and a long drying time between coats (about 24 to 48 hours between each coat). Spirit varnish only needs to dry for about 4 to 8 hours between each coat in warm, dry weather. Both of these types of varnish are available from luthier supply houses, and are applied in the same manner.

Application

To start, you will need to seal the wood. This is done by mixing some varnish with turpentine in a small jar, using about 20 percent varnish and 80 percent turpentine. The mixture will be very thin. Now brush this all over the instrument, starting at the top, using long smooth strokes and brushing with the grain until you get to the bottom. Now hang up the instrument to dry. Mix a larger batch of varnish this time, thinning it to 50 percent of its strength (half varnish and half turpentine). When the first coat is thoroughly dry, brush on the next coat in the same manner. Don't overload your brush and don't let the varnish run into drips. The varnish should be thin enough so that it flows into itself, leaving no brush marks as you go. Allow this coat to dry thoroughly before the next coat is applied. With oil varnish you will need 4 to 6 coats; for spirit varnish, 6 to 8 coats will do. When all the coats have been applied, the instrument must be put aside for the varnish to cure and harden. This takes two weeks for spirit varnish and about four to six weeks for oil varnish in warm, dry weather.

Rubbing Out The Finish

After the finish has hardened, it must be rubbed out; that is, streaks left by the brushing, drip marks, and any other faults in the finish must be evened out. These high spots are sanded off with No. 600 wet and dry sandpaper. At this point, all sanding is done with the sandpaper wet with water. When you have re-sanded, you will notice that while you have leveled the finish, you have also lost that high gloss and transparency. To get this back, you will need to mix powdered rotten stone and water into a liquid paste. This paste is then rubbed over the entire instrument with a felt pad until the high gloss returns.

Lacquer Finish

Before the instrument is sprayed with lacquer, it is sealed with lacquer sanding sealer. Buy the same brand of sanding sealer as the brand of lacquer you will use. The best brand of lacquer I have found is Sherman and Williams No. 600 Furniture Lacquer. DuPont also makes a good brand of lacquer. Now when the instrument is sanded all over, spray on a coat of sanding sealer. Allow this to dry about 1/2 hour, and then re-sand the entire instrument with fine sandpaper. Now mix your lacquer with an equal amount of lacquer thinner, fill your spray gun or air brush, and spray two to three coats, waiting about 1/2 hour between coats. Here are a few points to help you to perfect your spraying technique. Set your sprayer so that it will shoot a fine mist. As this mist hits the surface of your instrument, it forms beads on the surface. Spray only until these beads start to flow together, and move on before they start to run. When these beads are dry, they are not level but are wavy.

This effect is called "orange peel," because that is what the surface looks like. This in turn must be sanded smooth between coats. To do this sand with No. 400 wet and dry sandpaper that is wet with water. Don't sand so hard that you go through the finish, though. Repeat these steps of spraying and sanding for about eight to ten coats.

Rubbing Out The Finish

Now that the lacquer is applied, it is time to level it and bring it up to a high gloss. First, sand out all the "orange peel" with No. 400 wet and dry sandpaper, using water as a lubricant. Then sand out all the scratches left by the No. 400 sandpaper, using No. 600 wet and dry sandpaper with water. When this is done, rub the entire instrument with lacquer polishing compound and a felt rag until a nice gloss is achieved. You will now be ready to fit up and string your instrument.

French Polish

This is a very old method of finishing. It can be done the old way with shellac flakes, or the new way with rubbing lacquer.

If you are using shellac flakes, they will need to be mixed with methyl alcohol. This is done by filling a small jar about 1/3 full with flakes, then filling the jar to about 2/3 full with methyl alcohol. Place a small clean stone or ball bearing in the jar to help with the agitation. Shake the jar until all the shellac flakes are dissolved. The mixture is now ready for use.

MATERIALS FOR FRENCH POLISHING

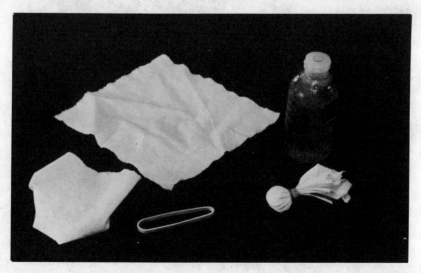

If you are using rubbing lacquer, there is no preliminary mixing. The best brand I have found is Qualasole, made by H. Behlen and Brothers Inc.

To apply French polish you will need two items. The first is a small plastic jar with the type of lid that has a small hole in the center that will let the liquid come out just a drop at a time. A druggist can supply this. The other item that you will need is a "rubber". This is made out of two pieces of lint free cloth measuring 4 inches by 4 inches, and a rubber band. One piece of the cloth is bundled up and then wrapped in the second, which is tied off with the rubber band. Now you are ready to finish your instrument.

French polishing is fairly easy to do. It's also kind of fun building up a nice finish. There are only three rules to remember: (1) when coming down on the surface of the instrument with the rubber, use a smooth sweeping motion like an airplane landing; (2) once on the surface, keep the rubber moving and don't stop it. If you do, there will be a blotch where you stop. Keep it moving smoothly in figure 8 patterns; (3) when you need to reload the rubber, lift it off the surface with an easy sweeping motion like an airplane taking off.

To break in your rubber, load it up well to start with. Then press it against the palm of your hand. It should be damp but not dripping. Start polishing with it and when it needs to have more polish put on it, add just two or three more drops. Keep this up until the finish is smooth all over and looks deep. After a few weeks, when the finish has hardened, it can be smoothed with No. 600 wet and dry sandpaper and then polished to a high gloss with rotten stone and water.

Vitali Import Co.
  5944-48 Atlantic Blvd., Maywood Calif.
  Tools, wood, books, and accessories. Catalog.

Marina Music
  1892 Union St. San Francisco, Calif.
  Wood, tools and accessories. Catalog.

J. F. Wallo
  1319 "F" street N. W., Washington D. C.
  Wood, tools, supplies. Catalog.

Underdog Music
  P. O. Box 1068, Willits, Calif.
  Wood, instrument supplies, kits, mail order catalog 50 cents.
H. Behlen and Bro. inc.
  Box 698, Amsterdam, New York 12010
  All wood finishing materials. Catalog.